Silvicultural Guide for Northern White-Cedar (Eastern White Cedar)

General Technical
Report NRS-98
2012

USDA United States
Department of Agriculture

Forest
Service

Northern
Research Station

ABSTRACT

Northern white-cedar (eastern white cedar; *Thuja occidentalis* L.) is an important tree species in the northeastern United States and adjacent Canada, occurring both in pure stands and as a minor species in mixed stands of hardwoods or other softwoods. Yet practitioners have little and often contradictory information about cedar ecology and silviculture. In response to this information need, a group of university and government researchers in the United States and Canada embarked on more than a decade of collaborative research; this guide is a compilation of the knowledge generated by that effort. It includes an overview of the commodity and non-commodity values of cedar, silvics of cedar and companion species, descriptions of the cedar resource in the northeastern United States, Quebec, and Ontario, and silvicultural guidelines based on previously published literature and new studies of cedar regeneration, growth, mortality, site relationships, and responses to treatment. With generally slow growth and little to no ingrowth on most inventory plots in the region, silvicultural prescriptions that explicitly address cedar are warranted. Recommendations include retaining and releasing cedar in managed stands, as well as establishing and protecting advance cedar regeneration and residual trees during harvesting. Partial cutting (e.g., the selection or irregular shelterwood method) is suggested for regenerating stands with a component of cedar, though browsing by white-tailed deer (*Odocoileus virginianus* Zimmermann) may influence treatment outcomes and must be considered. Once established, cedar responds well to release and will benefit from competition control and thinning. In mixed-species stands, within-stand flexibility of treatment is critical for maintaining cedar when other, more dominant species are driving silvicultural prescriptions at the stand level; a "micro-stand" approach in which pockets of cedar are identified and managed is suggested.

Cover Photos

Top left: Cones on cedar foliage. Photo by Sabrina Morissette, used with permission.
Bottom left: Cedar stand. Photo by Stéphane Tremblay, MRNF.
Top right: Cedar stand. Photo by Sabrina Morissette, used with permission.
Bottom right: Cedar seedlings. Photo by Elizabeth Larouche, MRNF.

Silvicultural Guide for
Northern White-Cedar (Eastern White Cedar)

Emmanuelle Boulfroy, Eric Forget, Philip V. Hofmeyer, Laura S. Kenefic,
Catherine Larouche, Guy Lessard, Jean-Martin Lussier, Fred Pinto,
Jean-Claude Ruel, and Aaron Weiskittel

U.S. Department of Agriculture, Forest Service
Northern Research Station
Newtown Square, PA
General Technical Report NRS-98
August 2012

Natural Resources   Ressources naturelles
Canada   Canada

Published in cooperation with
Natural Resources Canada
Canadian Forest Service

The participation of government employees in the
preparation of this document does not imply its
content represents government policy on cedar
management.

AUTHORS

Emmanuelle Boulfroy is a research forester, Centre d'enseignement et de recherche en foresterie de Sainte-Foy inc., 2424 Ste-Foy Road, Quebec, Quebec G1V 1T2.

Eric Forget is a forester, Nova Sylva inc., 147 Joseph Street, Gatineau, Quebec J8L 1G3.

Philip V. Hofmeyer is an assistant professor, Renewable Energy Training Center, Morrisville State College, Morrisville, NY 13408.

Laura S. Kenefic is a research forester, U.S. Department of Agriculture, Forest Service, Northern Research Station, Penobscot Experimental Forest, 686 Government Road, Bradley, ME 04411.

Catherine Larouche is a research scientist, Direction de la recherche forestière, Ministère des Ressources naturelles et de la Faune du Québec, 2700 Einstein Street, Quebec, Quebec G1P 3W8.

Guy Lessard is a research forester, Centre d'enseignement et de recherche en foresterie de Sainte-Foy inc., 2424 Ste-Foy Road, Quebec, Quebec G1V 1T2.

Jean-Martin Lussier is a research scientist, Natural Resources Canada - Canadian Wood Fibre Centre, 1055, du PEPS Street, Quebec, Quebec G1V 4C7.

Fred Pinto is an applied research forester, Southern Science and Information Section, Ministry of Natural Resources, 3301 Trout Lake Road, North Bay, Ontario P1A 4L7.

Jean-Claude Ruel is a silviculture professor, Département des sciences du bois et de la forêt, Faculté de foresterie, de géographie et de géomatique, Université Laval, 2405, de la Terrasse Street, Quebec, Quebec G1V 0A6.

Aaron Weiskittel is an assistant professor, School of Forest Resources, University of Maine, Orono, ME 04469.

CONTENTS

Despite its importance to biodiversity and use in a variety of products, northern white-cedar (eastern white cedar; *Thuja occidentalis* L., referred to as cedar throughout this guide) is often considered a secondary species. It is among the least studied commercially important tree species in North America. Forest practitioners encountering cedar have little or sometimes contradictory information about its characteristics and potential. The challenges of managing for multiple objectives makes it difficult to consider cedar in silvicultural prescriptions. As a result, silvicultural treatments are often inadequate to insure that cedar stands or the cedar components of mixed-species stands are renewed. This could diminish forest biodiversity and lead to a reduction in the sustainable level of cedar harvesting in the future.

For the last 10 years, professors and graduate students from the University of Maine (Orono, ME) and Laval University (Quebec, QC, Canada) have been working with government researchers from the United States and Canada to improve our understanding of the ecology and silviculture of cedar. The ultimate goal of these efforts was to create and publish this silviculture guide to help forest practitioners make decisions when managing cedar. Because most of the cedar range is found in Canada and the adjacent northeastern part of the United States, this guide has been developed by experts from both countries.

Developing a silviculture guide for a species that often occurs as a minor component of stands dominated by, and managed for, other species is very challenging. Instead of using a prescriptive approach, we opted to present key information about cedar and companion species likely to impact its success, and to allow forest managers to determine the best option for their specific situation. This guide applies to all stands with cedar, whether cedar is the dominant species or a minor component. It is applicable to forest practitioners on public or private land, or to woodlot owners, anywhere in eastern Canada and United States.

Due to its slow growth, the diversity of ecosystems it occupies, and the fact that it is highly palatable to white-tailed deer (*Odocoileus virginianus* Zimmermann, referred to as deer throughout this guide) and other browsing mammals, cedar can be difficult to manage. We hope this guide will be a useful tool for forest managers in both countries.

A French version of this guide will be published by the Canadian Forest Service. *Une version française de ce guide sera publiée par le Service canadien des forêts.*

Why Manage for Cedar?

Cedar is often a minor component of mixed-species stands and is harvested opportunistically during operations aimed at more abundant species. Lack of attention to cedar silviculture has had negative impacts throughout its range. Cedar trees harvested in mixed stands are often replaced by more abundant and competitive companion species, resulting in compositional shifts (57). Reductions in the abundance of cedar have been reported for whole regions of Quebec (13, 74). In southern Ontario, cedar has become less dominant within stands while at the same time there are fewer cedar stands overall (111). Cedar harvest exceeds growth in some areas of the northeastern United States (88).

Does it matter if the amount of cedar is reduced, or if we fail to recruit new cedar trees? Yes, for many reasons. Cedar has important economic, social, and spiritual values. From a commodity-production perspective, between 275,000 to 350,000 m^3 (115,000 to 150,000 cords) of cedar are harvested and transformed into products each year in the New England states, Ontario, and Quebec (32, 65, 87). This represents $15 to $20 million (U.S. dollars) annually in mill-delivered log revenues alone. Cedar contributes importantly to niche markets for specialty products such as shingles and fence posts and is a prime species for the production of appearance-grade lumber, garden components, exterior furniture, and many other products. Most of the cedar processing residues are utilized in mulch production. As a result, the harvesting and transformation of cedar support communities dependent on forest management and forest products manufacturing.

Cedar also has many noncommodity values. It is one of the sacred plants for Native Americans (39). It is widely recognized for its potential to produce nontimber forest products such as medicines and essential oils. Cedar also is an important contributor to biodiversity by increasing local tree species richness, providing wildlife habitat (47), and increasing vertical structure through its unique crown form (141) and vegetative reproduction through layering (71). Cedar is extremely long-lived and has few insect pests; it has potential for management for late-successional or old-growth forest characteristics (46). Pure cedar stands can occur on wet or highly disturbed sites (81), and thus play an important role in maintaining forest cover in areas unsuited to other tree species.

Cedar provides critical winter habitat for deer (131) and increasing deer populations in many parts of the region have resulted in recruitment failures (135). This endangers both sustainability of the cedar resource and habitat quality, especially in deer wintering areas (DWAs). While excluding these stands or the cedar within them from harvest protects existing cedar, it does little to improve the growth and vigor of those stems or recruit new trees or stands for future habitat (31, 136). Unmanaged stands of pure cedar have been observed to have a low rate of canopy disturbance, with little recruitment of new trees (44). Appropriate silvicultural treatments within DWAs can improve tree vigor and increase recruitment, without degrading existing habitat values.

For these reasons, it is important that management plans and silvicultural prescriptions, including those for mixed stands dominated by other species, be modified to maintain a cedar component. It is our responsibility as forest stewards to sustain this species and its myriad ecological and social values.

Wood Properties

Cedar is a valuable and desired species for the production of many commercial products. Cedar has weak physical properties, beautiful light brown color, good wood-working properties, and remarkable natural durability (Table 1).

Cedar wood accepts adhesives readily from a wide range of glues and take stains well. Painting quality is very good.

Cedar products are very durable and require little maintenance. The wood contains natural preservatives that protect it from rot and insects after harvesting. Unlike other species that contain tannins, cedar can be stained just about every color imaginable, from palest to darkest, making it a preferred choice for a number of home uses (e.g., shingle wall siding, playground equipment, decks, and flower boxes).

Due to its exceptionally high natural resistance to decay, the wood of cedar is processed into lumber and shingles and used for applications where it is exposed to a high decay hazard, e.g., paneling, boats, greenhouses, and outdoor furniture. Cedar logs are also processed into products that withstand

Table 1.—Physical and wood-working properties of cedar

Properties	Values	
Physical properties		
Color	Heartwood[a]: light brown Sapwood[b]: almost white (16)	
Density	The weakest among companion species[c]: 340 kg/m^3 (21.23 lbs/ft^3) (67)	
Static bending:		
modulus of rupture[d] (MOR) 12% modulus of elasticity[e] (MOE) 12%	MOR: The weakest among companion species: 4.31 kg/mm^2 (6,130 lb/in^2) MOE: The weakest among companion species: 446 kg/mm^2 (635,000 lb/in^2) (67)	
Wood-working properties (85) (% success[f]; relative success[g])		
Planing	71; Moderate-high	
Sanding	94; Very high	
Drilling	Double margin drill bit: 100; Very high Tooth drill bit: 68; Moderate	
Mortise	56; Moderate	
Moulding	60; Moderate-high	
Turning	98; Very high	

[a] The inner, nonliving part of a tree stem that is altered to a protective state as a result of normal, genetically controlled aging processes as cells die, and that provides mechanical support (130).

[b] The outer layers of a stem, which in a live tree are composed of living cells and conduct water up the tree. Note: sapwood is generally lighter in color than heartwood (130).

[c] See Table 5 for list of companion species.

[d] A measure of the maximum wood fiber stress at failure (compression or tension) under an applied bending load (130).

[e] A measure of wood deformation under an applied load equal to the ratio of stress to strain within the elastic range (when strain is proportional to the applied stress) (130).

[f] The % success is the rating for cedar.

[g] The relative success is based on the rating for cedar compared to the ratings of the companion species.

degradation from water and soil, such as fence posts and pilings (71).

The effects of silviculture on wood properties of cedar are unknown.

Log Characteristics and Other Cedar Usage

Different end products require different log qualities and characteristics. The value of cedar logs depends on their size (length and diameter), quality (based on the presence or absence of defects or characteristics such as knots, rot, sweep, crook, fork, bird or insect holes, ring shake, and moisture content), and the market demand. A cubic meter of cedar in 2010 was worth between $18 and $100 U.S. ($40 and $240 U.S./cord) delivered to the mill, depending on log quality (Table 2) and market demand.

Cedar mulch, typically in landscaping and decorating, also has several benefits besides aesthetics. Mulch prevents the growth of competitive weeds, maintains ground moisture, and provides insulation during the colder season.

Cedar boughs and cones are used to create wreathes, potpourri, and sachets. Shredded cedar bark makes an excellent fire starter. Traditionally, the inner bark of cedar was used as a fiber for making rope and fabric

Table 2.—Utilization chart and value for cedar logs

Utilization	Log quality	Log size	Log value (2010 U.S. dollars)
Interior moulding, panelling, carpenter grade, exterior siding	100% sound and straight (no defects) 100% sound and straight Sound and tight knots tolerated	Small end diameter (inside bark): ≥ 15 cm (6 in) Length: ≥ 1.85 m (6 ft)	± $80/m³ ± $200/cord
Shingle	Logs of 22 cm (8.5 in) to 40 cm (16 in) in diameter: Minimum of 10 cm (4 in) of sound peripheral wood on 3 faces (can tolerate up to 50% heart rot content) Logs ≥ 40 cm (16 in) in diameter: Minimum of 13 cm (5 in) of sound peripheral wood on three faces (can tolerate up to 50% heart rot content) Minimal restriction on sweep	Small end diameter (inside bark): ≥ 22 cm (8.5 in) Length: ≥ 2.65 m (8 ft 8 in)	± $65/m³ ± $155/cord
Outdoor furniture, garden and landscaping components, fencing components	100% sound and straight (no defects)	Small end diameter (inside bark): ≥ 13 cm (5 in) Length: ≥ 1.85 m (6 ft)	± $60/m³ ± $145/cord
Post	Sound and straight	Small end diameter (inside bark): ≥ 5 cm (2 in) Length: ≥ 1.85 m (6 ft)	
Mulch	Any logs that do not meet the above-mentioned criteria Cedar sawmill production residues	Any size	± $18/m³ ± $43/cord

(5). Cedar boughs are harvested and distilled to create an essential oil, which is used as a moth repellent and an ingredient in household cleansers and cosmetics.

Pharmacological Properties

Cedar has immuno-stimulating and antiviral potentials. In combination with other immunomodulating plants such as coneflower (*Echinacea purpurea* [L.] Moench and *Echinacea pallida* [Nutt.] Nutt.) and wild indigo (*Baptisia tinctoria* [Bapt.]), cedar is used as phytotherapy for upper respiratory infections and as an adjuvant to antibiotics in bacterial infections such as bronchitis, angina pharyngitis, otitis media, and sinusitis (96).

The oil from cedar is also one of the principal ingredients in many commercial and alternative medicines, including cold remedies (39). A critical factor for cedar's use as a medicinal herb is its high content of thujone (65 percent of the essential oil of the fresh leaves), which is reported to be a toxic agent. Thujone can cause vomiting, stomach ache, diarrhea, and gastroenteritis as well as absorption disorders, nervous agitation and chronic convulsions, and symptoms of liver and renal toxicity (96).

Native Values

Cedar is considered an important resource for cultural and traditional purposes and is one of the four sacred medicines used by many North American native peoples. It has been used for centuries for medicinal purposes in a variety of ways including consuming an infusion of the leaves or inner bark as cough medicine, and inhaling the steam or vapors in sweat lodges to combat colds, headache, fever, and rheumatism (39). Its vitamin C content helped prevent scurvy (37) when fruit and vegetables were unavailable during the winter months (82). Cedar is also burned during prayer and meditation ceremonies for cleansing, clearing, and blessing.

Native people long ago recognized the unique properties of the cedar. Taking advantage of its light weight and decay resistance, wood strips of cedar were used to build the frame of white birch (*Betula papyrifera* Marsh.) canoes (82).

Jacques Cartier, the first European to reach Canada, mentioned in his travel log that during the winter of 1534-35 in Stadacona (Quebec City), he treated his crew affected by scurvy with a cedar bark decoction recommended by Native Americans (11).

Importance of Cedar for Biodiversity

Maintaining biodiversity is a key component of sustainable forest management. Cedar contributes to nontimber forest values because of its longevity (2), unique stem form and crown structure (140), tendency to decay when living (60), resistance to rot as a snag (47) or downed log, and occurrence as a minor species in stands dominated by other species.

Structure and Composition

Individual cedar trees can live for a very long time and cedar stands often exist in areas that have not had recent stand-replacing disturbances (80). As such, cedar stands may be associated with late successional or rare species; 17 rare plants are known to be associated with cedar swamps and seepage forests in Maine (17), and many cedar-associated plants species are listed as endangered or threatened in several states or provinces (Table 3). Cedar also contributes to tree species richness as a minor component of mixed-species stands within its range.

Cedar trees maintain more of their foliage lower in the crown than associated conifers (140), and thus contribute to vertical stratification of the canopy. Cedar is also highly resistant to decay after mortality and persists as dead wood for much longer than other species (47).

Table 3.—Endangered or threatened plants associated with cedar in northeastern United States (97), Ontario (106), and Quebec (34)

Common name	Scientific name
Roundleaf orchid	*Amerorchis rotundifolia* (Banks ex Pursh) Hultén
Fairy slipper	*Calypso bulbosa* (L.) Oakes
Showy lady's slipper	*Cypripedium reginae* Walter
Hooded coralroot	*Corallorhiza striata* Lindl. var. striata
Walking fern	*Asplenium rhizophyllum* L.
Ram's head lady's slipper	*Cypripedium arietinum* W.T. Aiton
New Jersey tea	*Ceanothus americanus* L.

Deer Wintering Areas

The winter survival of deer at the northern extent of its range is directly related to the availability and quality of habitat in deer wintering areas (DWAs): softwood-dominated stands with a high, mostly closed canopy. These stands provide food and cover for deer during the winter when deep snow inhibits browsing and travel and energy expenditures are high. Forest managers must be aware of local DWA regulations, which define acceptable canopy height and canopy closure, season of operation, and softwood species composition. The constraints posed by these regulations, and by the habitat needs of deer, may limit the silvicultural treatments that can be applied.

Wildlife Habitat

Mature cedar trees and old stands provide preferred habitat for more than half the vertebrate species living in cedar stands of the boreal and the Great Lakes-St. Lawrence forest regions (64).

Deer, moose (*Alces alces* Gray), and snowshoe hare (*Lepus americanus* Erxleben) browse cedar and use it as shelter in the winter. Lowland cedar in the boreal forest region is considered preferred breeding habitat for 21 bird species and one mammal, and supports year-round use by boreal chickadees (*Poecile hudsonicus* Forster) and three mammals (64) (Fig. 1). Upland cedar in the boreal forest region is preferred breeding habitat for 20 bird species and is used by two bird and six mammal species all year (64). Further south, in the Great Lakes-St. Lawrence forest region, lowland cedar is preferred breeding habitat for 23 birds and one mammal (*Lynx canadensis* Kerr) species, while upland cedar is the preferred breeding habitat for 17 bird and one mammal species (64). Great Lakes-St. Lawrence forest region cedar stands further provide preferred habitat all year for an additional three bird and eight mammal species.

Figure 1.—Cedar north of Gatineau, Quebec. Photo by Eric Forget, Nova Sylva Inc., used with permission.

Genetic Diversity

Cedar is morphologically similar throughout its range, with no races or varieties reported. But a rangewide provenance study indicates that significant genetic variation does exist (71). Upland and lowland ecotypes were found within a kilometer of each other in Wisconsin (95), but the extent of differentiation is not well documented. No natural or artificial hybrids have been reported.

In the absence of data on the adaptive traits of cedar, it may be a good policy to use local seed provenances for plantations. However, if climate change is believed likely to occur it would be preferable to choose seed provenances with consideration to climate change. Because of the lack of data on cedar genetics, the best alternative would be to base the choice of seed provenances on the behavior of associated, better documented conifer species, like white spruce (*Picea glauca* [Moench] Voss) and black spruce (*Picea mariana* [Mill.] B.S.P.).

Cedar often reproduces and regenerates in stands with low-intensity disturbances that create small gaps in the forest canopy (9, 22), or where catastrophic stand-replacing disturbances are infrequent (139, 143) (Fig. 2). Susceptibility and vulnerability of cedar trees to these and other natural disturbances are influenced by a number of factors. The morphology of cedar, with its crown low to the ground (140) and thin stringy bark, suggests a high probability of mortality from fire. In addition, cedar's weak wood (8) makes it susceptible to wind, ice, and snow damage, particularly when the heartwood is attacked by fungi. Breakages can cause permanent stem deformation (115). However, these disturbances are likely to create high levels of decaying wood on the forest floor, which may facilitate cedar reproduction (26, 28). Dead cedar trees also become long-lived snags (47) that play a role in creating structural features and wildlife habitat.

The small openings created by single or groups of trees dying may be filled by advance regeneration from cedar, which is adapted to producing seedling banks (77). Cedar seedlings and saplings are able to survive for long periods in the understory if wildlife browsing is low, improving their chances of recruiting into the overstory.

Cedar heartwood is frequently attacked by fungi. Cedar trees on xeric and basic sites have a moderate resistance to decay, whereas cedar on acid and wet sites have a very low resistance (14). Redheart rot, caused by *Stereum sanguinolentum*, is a common disease of the bole. The fungus penetrates wounds on the bole, dead branches, branches, or forks broken by heavy snow or ice, or the wounds created by pruning. Old trees are often affected by red-brown butt rot (*Coniophora puteana*, *Phaeolus schweinitzii*)

Figure 2.—Blowdown in a cedar stand north of Gatineau, Quebec. Photo by Eric Forget, Nova Sylva Inc., used with permission.

and stringy butt rot (*Odontia bicolor*, *Perenniporia subacida*, *Scytinostroma galactinum*) (4, 14).

Carpenter ants (*Camponotus* sp.) frequently attack partially decayed heartwood in living trees (15). Leafminers (*Argyresthia* sp., *Pulicalvaria* sp.) are common and cause the leaves to wither and turn brown, reducing growth and leading to death (118).

Operational observations and research (10, 25, 77, 136) indicate that ungulate and hare browsing are major factors reducing the ability of this species to recruit into the overstory. Uncontrolled logging and selective removal of cedar are also speculated as causing declines in cedar abundance across whole regions in Quebec and Ontario (13, 111).

Cedar

The native range of cedar extends through the southern part of the eastern half of Canada and the adjacent northern part of the United States (Fig. 3). In Canada, this species grows from southeastern Manitoba to the southern part of Nova Scotia. In the United States, it extends from Minnesota to Maine, and all the way to Tennessee and South Carolina. It is considered critically imperiled in several states, including Illinois, Indiana, New Jersey, and Massachusetts (98).

Table 4 presents cedar habitat, reproduction, growth, and stress factors. Appendix I provides quantitative information on growth and yield.

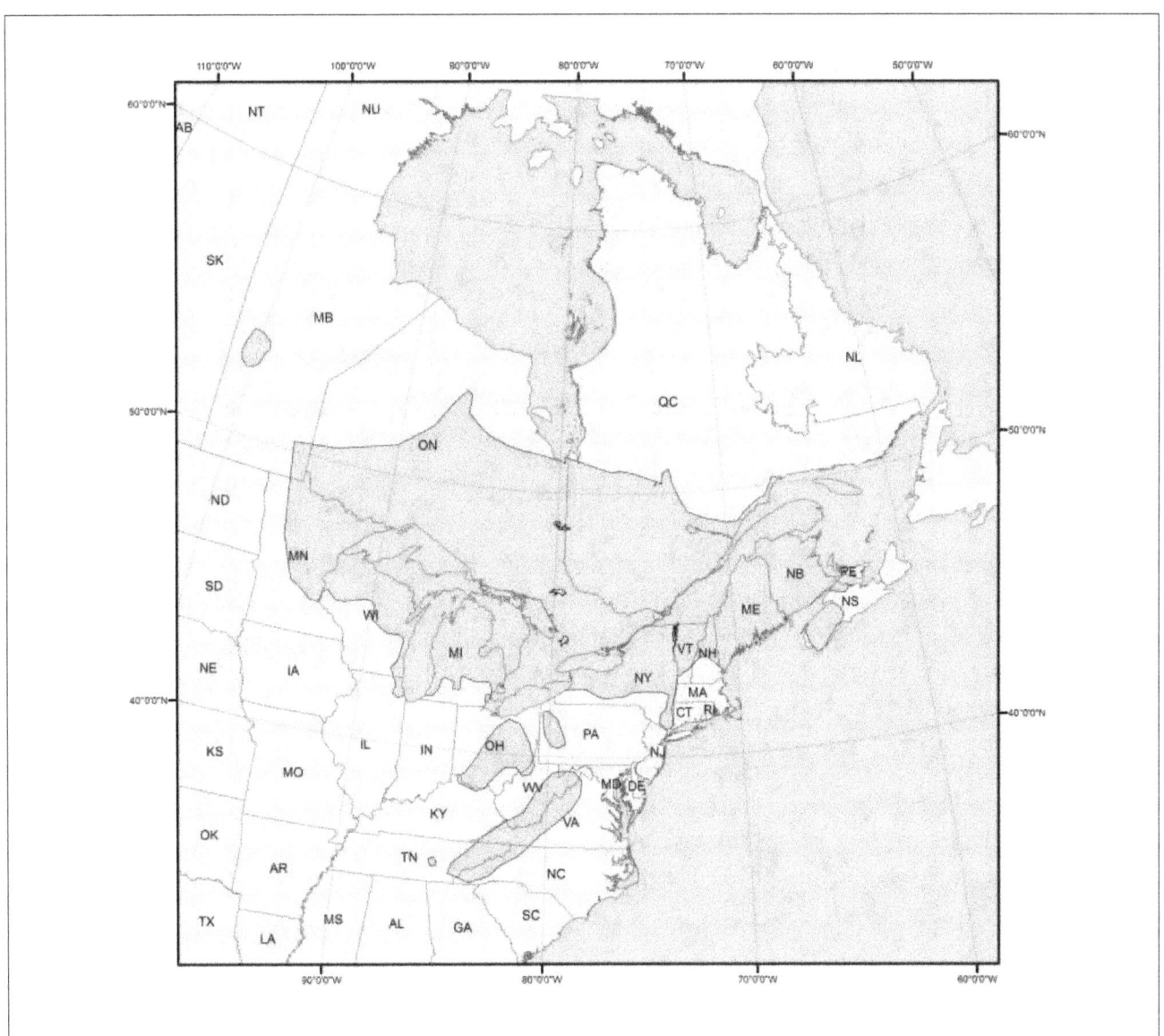

Figure 3.—Cedar distribution (in pink). Figure by Eric Forget, Nova Sylva, based on [71], used with permission.

Table 4.—Habitat, dynamics, reproduction, growth, and stress factors for cedar

Characteristics	Factors	References
Habitat		
Physical environment	All topographic locations	58, 71, 72
	More frequent in depressions and imperfectly to very poorly drained soils (lower level of competition)	
	All drainage and soil texture	
	Best growth on fine textured and well drained soils with seepage	
	Often found on calcareous soils: Growth and health positively correlated with Ca and Mg availability, which gives cedar a competitive advantage on the very fertile soils of the clay belt in Quebec and Ontario	
	Growth and health negatively correlated with acidity and aluminum	
Dynamic		
Sociology	Generally clumped in mixed stands	21, 71, 91
	As pure stands on poorly drained soils, poor sites	
Shade tolerance	Seedlings: mid-tolerant	21, 71, 122
	Layering regeneration: very tolerant	
	Mature trees: tolerant to very tolerant	
Reproduction - regeneration initiation		
Reproduction mode		
Reproduction	Layering on poorly drained (organic soils) or very well drained sites	9, 71, 91, 136
	Layering or sexual reproduction on moderately well drained sites	
Vegetative reproduction	Layering: plentiful (except in dense stands); can send roots from any part of a branch or stem if moisture conditions are favorable	9, 21, 71, 76, 91, 136
	Seedlings may produce layering at an early age (5 years)	
Seed production and dispersal		
Sexual maturity	20-30 years	21, 71, 93, 122
Age for optimal seed production	75 years and older	21, 71
Frequency of good seed crops	2-5 years	50, 71, 76, 91
Time of seed dispersal	August to mid-October	71
Seed dispersion distance (and mode)	45 to 60 m (147.6 to 196.8 ft) (wind)	71, 91, 93
	Optimal: < 20 m (65.6 ft)	
Duration of seed viability	In soil: < 1 year	71
	In cones: < 1 year	
Loss of seed through diseases and predators	Low	48

(Table 4 continued on next page)

Table 4 (continued).—Habitat, dynamics, reproduction, growth, and stress factors for cedar

Characteristics	Factors	References
Reproduction - regeneration initiation (continued)		
Establishment		
Water requirements	Humid substrate (limiting factor)	25, 71
Light requirements	Partial (50% crown closure)	79, 104
Preferred seedbed	Decaying (rotten) wood of logs and stumps > mineral soil > burnt organic matter	27, 57, 71, 104, 124, 128
	Elevated microtopographical feature (hummock, decaying wood)	
	Limited survival on undisturbed humus and thick layer of feathermoss	
Seedlings and saplings development and growth		
Water requirements	Seedlings: high (constant moisture supply); more limiting than light	25, 71, 79
	Saplings: moderate	
Light requirements	Partial (~50% crown closure): best growth (tallest seedlings)	71
	Full light: heaviest shoots and roots	
Growth	Seedlings: very slow; height growth 1-4 cm/yr (0.4-1.6 in/yr); up to 15 cm/yr (5.9 in/yr) in optimal conditions; diameter growth at the collar 1-4 mm/yr (0.04-0.16 in/yr); at least 11 years to reach 30 cm (11.8 in) of height; at least 14 to 32 years to reach 1.3 m (4.3 ft) of height	60-62, 76, 79
	Saplings: slow; average height growth of 4-8 cm/yr (1.6-3.1 in/yr); about 100 years to grow from a dbh of 1.3 to 11.4 cm (0.5-4.5 in)	
Response to release	Good, can withstand severe suppression for several years	71, 76, 124
Sensitivity to competition for light and soil resources	Seedlings: moderate	76
	Saplings: low	
Main damaging agents	Browsing by deer (for stems 20 cm [7.9 in] to 2 m [6.6 ft] tall)	28, 71, 75, 77
Stress tolerance and resistance	Freezing resistance: low (seedlings)	71, 76, 117
	Drought resistance: low (seedlings)	
Mortality rates	Seedlings: very high during the early years (drought and damage including smothering by sphagnum moss or logging slash)	28, 58, 71, 78
	Saplings: high with constant browsing, otherwise low	

(Table 4 continued on next page)

Table 4 (continued).—Habitat, dynamics, reproduction, growth, and stress factors for cedar

Characteristics	Factors	References
Growth of mature trees		
Site index (Height at age 50)	Quebec: mean variability range = 8.2-10.4 m (27-34 ft)	24, 121
	Ontario (Boreal forest): mean = 8.5 m (28 ft)	
	NE U.S.: mean ± standard deviation = 8.9 ± 2.4 m (29.2 ± 7.9 ft)	
Absolute rotation age (based on the maximum value of Mean Annual Increment of merchantable volume for a dbh of 9 cm) per relative density (low, medium, and high relative density)	Site index 9: 150, 115, 85 (Quebec)	112
Typical natural longevity	400 years	40, 71, 102, 122
Range of average diameter growth	Quebec: Crown closure > 60%: 1.34-1.86 mm/yr Crown closure < 60%: 2.08-2.36 mm/yr	24, 94
	Ontario (Boreal forest): 0.8 mm/yr	
	NE U.S.: 2 ± 1.4 mm/yr	
Response to release	Good, even for older trees	21, 71, 78
Stress factors - Stress tolerance and resistance		
Wind firmness	Low on very wet soils or following canopy opening Otherwise good	102
Resistance to ice rain, ice, and snow	Low (breakage) Permanent bole deformation	15, 21, 71
Drought resistance	Low to moderate on imperfectly drained soils High on calcareous soils	59
Tolerance to flooding and high water tables	Low to moderate: reduced growth rate and death of entire stands if restricted soil aeration resulting from abnormally high water levels	21, 59, 71
Tolerance to soil compaction	Moderate to high	59, 66
Other important stress factors	Bark slipping	71
Main damages from animals	Bole: bears, woodpeckers Browsing by deer, moose, and hare	4, 15, 71, 104

Companion species

The principal species associated with cedar in the northeastern United States, Quebec, and Ontario are balsam fir (*Abies balsamea* [L.] Mill.), white spruce, red spruce (*Picea rubens* [Sarg.]), black spruce, and eastern hemlock (*Tsuga canadensis* [L.] Carrière).

Hardwood companion species are red maple (*Acer rubrum* L.), sugar maple (*Acer saccharum* Marsh.), yellow birch (*Betula alleghaniensis* Britton), paper birch, and trembling aspen (*Populus tremuloides* L.) (Table 5).

Table 5.—Comparison of the shade tolerance, reproduction and regeneration, and growth for cedar and ten other companion species

Species	Dynamic		Reproduction and Regeneration Initiation		
	Shade Tolerance		Preferred reproduction method	Periodicity of good seed production (years)	Preferred seedbed
Eastern white cedar, Northern white-cedar	Seedlings (no tol. — mid tol. — tolerant — very tol.; mid-tolerant range) Layers (no tol. — mid tol. — tolerant — very tol.; tolerant to very tolerant range) Saplings and mature trees (no tol. — mid tol. — tolerant — very tol.; tolerant range)		• Vegetative (layering) on poorly drained and dry soils • Vegetative (layering) or sexual on moderately well drained soils • Advance regeneration	2-5	• Rotting wood, mineral soil, litter, burnt humus
Balsam fir	no tol. mid tol. tolerant very tol. (tolerant range)		• Sexual • Advance regeneration	2-4	• Mineral soil, mosses, rotting wood
White spruce	no tol. mid tol. tolerant very tol. (mid-tolerant range)		• Sexual • Advance regeneration	2-6	• Rich mineral soil, mineral soil and organic matter mixture, rotting wood
Black spruce	no tol. mid tol. tolerant very tol. (mid to tolerant range)		• Usually vegetative (layering) • Sexual after fire - on bare or exposed mineral soil	4	• Humus, mineral soil, mineral soil and organic matter mixture, sphagnum
Red spruce	no tol. mid tol. tolerant very tol. (tolerant range)		• Sexual	3-8	• Rotting wood, mosses, conifer leaf litter, mineral soil and organic matter mixture, mineral soil
Eastern hemlock	no tol. mid tol. tolerant very tol. (tolerant range)		• Sexual	2-3	• Mineral soil, mineral soil and organic matter mixture, burnt litter and humus, rotting wood, stump
Red maple	no tol. mid tol. tolerant very tol. (mid-tolerant range)		• Vegetative (sprout) or sexual • Advance regeneration	2	• Mineral soil, a wide range of seed beds
Sugar maple	no tol. mid tol. tolerant very tol. (tolerant range)		• Sexual • Advance regeneration	3-7	• A wide range of seed beds (from leaf litter to bare mineral soil)
Yellow birch	no tol. mid tol. tolerant very tol. (mid-tolerant range)		• Sexual	2-3	• Mineral soil, mineral soil and organic matter mixture, rotting wood, litter and burnt humus
Paper birch, White birch	no tol. mid tol. tolerant very tol. (no tolerance range)		• Usually sexual	2-3	• Mineral soil, rotting wood, mineral soil and organic matter mixture
Trembling aspen	no tol. mid tol. tolerant very tol. (no tolerance range)		• Usually vegetative (root sucker) • From seeds on bare or exposed mineral soils	4-5	• Mineral soils, humus, burnt litter and humus

(Table 5 continued on next page)

Table 5 (continued).—Comparison of the shade tolerance, reproduction and regeneration, and growth for cedar and ten other companion species

Species	Seedlings and Saplings Development and Growth			
	Growth	Response to canopy openings	Sensitivity to competition	Mortality
Eastern white cedar, Northern white-cedar	Seedlings very slow slow moderate fast Saplings very slow slow moderate fast	• Good (even after a long suppression period)	Seedlings low moderate high very high Saplings low moderate high very high	• Seedlings: very high during the early years • Saplings: high with persistent browsing, otherwise low
Balsam fir	very slow slow moderate fast Slow growth but faster than white and red spruces	• Very good (even after a long suppression period)	low moderate high very high	• Low after one year • High in open environment
White spruce	very slow slow moderate fast	• Good (even after a long suppression period, but must be well established) • Better between ages 20 and 40	low moderate high very high	• High for year 1 and 2, and decreasing after
Black spruce	Seedlings very slow slow moderate fast Saplings very slow slow moderate fast	• Good (even after a long suppression period)	Seedlings low moderate high very high Saplings low moderate high very high	• Layers: 20% in year 1, and decreases sharply onward • Seedlings: high in year 1, <10% after year 3
Red spruce	very slow slow moderate fast	• Good if gradual opening (even after a long suppression period)	Seedlings low moderate high very high Saplings low moderate high very high	• High if seedlings <15 cm • Very high in open environment
Eastern hemlock	Seedlings very slow slow moderate fast Saplings very slow slow moderate fast	• Good if gradual opening	low moderate high very high	Best survival on moss and where herb cover is denser
Red maple	very slow slow moderate fast	• Good	low moderate high very high	• Seedlings: high under a dense canopy • Constant renewal of the seedling bank

(Table 5 continued on next page)

Table 5 (continued).—Comparison of the shade tolerance, reproduction and regeneration, and growth for cedar and ten other companion species

Species	Seedlings and Saplings Development and Growth				
	Growth	Response to canopy openings	Sensitivity to competition	Mortality
Sugar maple	very slow — slow — moderate — fast (slow–moderate)	• Good (until age 30)	low — moderate — high — very high (moderate)	• Seedlings: 50% during year 1, decreases in seedlings of 25 cm or less in height • High under a dense canopy (<5 years)
Yellow birch	very slow — slow — moderate — fast (moderate)	• Good	low — moderate — high — very high (moderate)	• High if exposed to drought, frost, browsing or if crushed by leaves
Paper birch, White birch	Seedlings: very slow — slow — moderate — fast (moderate) Sprouts: very slow — slow — moderate — fast (fast)	• Very good and fast	Seedlings: low — moderate — high — very high (moderate) Saplings: low — moderate — high — very high (high)	• High under canopy
Trembling aspen	Seedlings: very slow — slow — moderate — fast (fast) Suckers: v. slow — slow — moderate — fast — very fast (fast)	• N/A: can't stand being under canopy	Seedlings: low — moderate — high — very high (high) Saplings: low — moderate — high — very high (high)	• Seedlings: high if exposed to drought • Saplings: high if intraspecific competition

(Table 5 continued on next page)

Table 5 (continued).—Comparison of the shade tolerance, reproduction and regeneration, and growth for cedar and ten other companion species

Species	Longevity (years)	Growth of Mature Trees		Response to canopy openings	Main references
		Average diameter increment (mm/year) by crown closure (CC) (Quebec data)	Percentile[a] of diameter increment (mm/year) (Maine, Quebec, Nova Scotia and New Brunswick data)		
Eastern white cedar, Northern white-cedar	>400	CC > 60%: 1.34-1.86 CC < 60%: 2.08-2.36	25 p: 1.06 50 p: 2.00 75 p: 2.53	Good at all stages	21, 57, 71, 76, 78, 103, 104, 124, 140
Balsam fir	150	CC > 60%: 1.58-2.25 CC < 60%: 2.08-2.96	25 p: 1.00 50 p: 2.00 75 p: 3.00	Good	21, 42, 102, 104, 105, 140
White spruce	>200	CC > 60%: 1.64-2.11 CC < 60%: 2.77-3.04	25 p: 1.20 50 p: 2.33 75 p: 3.80	Good at all stages	40, 100, 103, 104, 140
Black spruce	175-200	CC > 60%: 0.99-1.44 CC < 60%: 1.15-1.88	25 p: 0.67 50 p: 1.33 75 p: 2.40	Good	21, 90, 102, 104, 105, 107, 113, 129, 140
Red spruce	>200	CC > 60%: 1.50-1.83 CC < 60%: 2.11-2.19	25 p: 1.20 50 p: 2.28 75 p: 3.38	Very good if partial opening	12, 21, 36, 104, 140
Eastern hemlock	>400	2.12-2.58	25 p: 1.60 50 p: 2.53 75 p: 3.81	Good if partial opening	21, 49, 93, 102, 104, 140, 142
Red maple	80	CC > 60%: 1.70-2.69 CC < 60%: 2.01-2.69	25 p: 1.00 50 p: 1.80 75 p: 2.67	Good to very good	103, 104, 137, 140
Sugar maple	300-350	CC > 60%: 1.83-2.99 CC < 60%: 2.08-3.70	25 p: 1.00 50 p: 2.00 75 p: 2.80	Moderate	21, 51, 86, 93, 104, 140
Yellow birch	>300	CC > 60%: 1.92-2.90 CC < 60%: 2.85-3.45	25 p: 1.20 50 p: 2.00 75 p: 3.12	Good; decreases with age	21, 38, 86, 93, 103-105, 140
Paper birch, White birch	<125-200	CC > 60%: 0.70-1.74 CC < 60%: 0.78-2.58	25 p: 0.67 50 p: 1.40 75 p: 2.31	Decreases with age	68, 93, 103, 104, 120, 140
Trembling aspen	100	CC > 60%: 1.65-3.06 CC < 60%: 2.09-3.59	25 p: 1.40 50 p: 2.60 75 p: 4.11	Good	21, 104, 108, 110, 140

[a] A percentile is the value below which a certain percentage of observations fall. In the first case, 25 p means that 25 percent of the cedar measured had a diameter increment of less than 1.06 mm/yr.

In Quebec

Cedar can be found in Quebec in the sugar maple-yellow birch and balsam fir-yellow birch climatic domains and the eastern balsam fir-paper birch climatic sub-domain. Even though it is widespread below the province's 48th parallel (Fig. 3), cedar exists in only about 15 percent of the stands in its natural range. The total volume of cedar in Quebec in 2010 was estimated at 102 million m³.[1] About 35 million m³ are located on private lands and 67 million on public land. About 6 million m³ are in unmanaged forests. As a ubiquitous species, cedar colonizes a wide range

[1]Extrapolation based on permanent sample plots.

of edaphic conditions but only some of them provide optimal growth. The proportion of cedar can vary greatly among stands (Fig. 4); it may be a minor species or in pure stands.

Sites in which cedar is the dominant species (>50 percent of basal area) are usually flat ground or depressions where water supplies nutrients that improve growing conditions of very poorly drained organic soils (Fig. 5). In those stands, the main companion species are balsam fir; black, red and white spruces; and paper birch (ecological types [52-56]: RC38, RS18). On rare occasions, cedar can be found

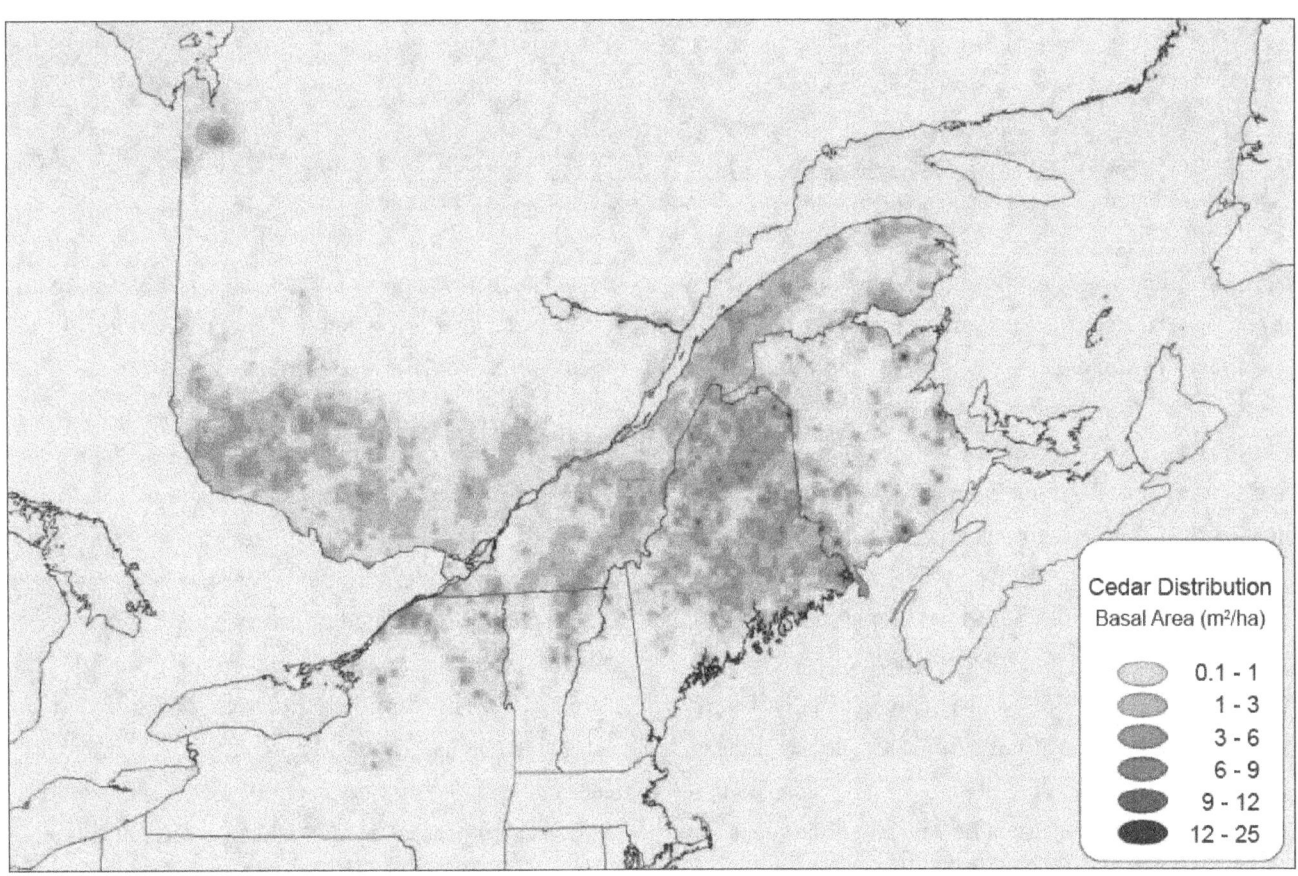

Cedar Distribution
Basal Area (m²/ha)

- 0.1 - 1
- 1 - 3
- 3 - 6
- 6 - 9
- 9 - 12
- 12 - 25

Figure 4.—Cedar basal area (m²/ha) in Quebec, Atlantic provinces, and northeastern United States. See Figure 6 for cedar distribution in Ontario. Eric Forget, Nova Sylva, used with permission.

Figure 5.—Cedar in Temiscamingue, Quebec. Photo by Sabrina Morissette, used with permission.

as the dominant species on well drained or imperfectly drained soils. Cedar is the dominant species in about 20 percent of stands.

Cedar is a significant companion species (between 25 and 50 percent of basal area) in about 20 percent of the stands where it occurs in Quebec. On well drained soils, cedar can be found with balsam fir, yellow birch, sugar maple, paper birch, and red maple (ecological types: RS12, RS13). On lower slopes or mid-slopes with imperfectly drained soils, cedar is usually found with a higher proportion of coniferous species (balsam fir, red spruce), even though hardwood species such as birch can also be present (main ecological types: RS15, RS16). Along streams or within depressions with good water supply, cedar can be found with other species such as balsam fir, black ash, trembling aspen, yellow and paper birch, and red maple (ecological types: MJ28, MF18).

In Quebec, the most common situation is sites in which cedar is a minor species (<25 percent of basal area). The wide range of sites can be very dry, calcareous soils of escarpments, on poorly drained soils, and on well drained or imperfectly drained soils. In these cases, cedar is mixed with a variety of tree species in coniferous-, mixed-, or hardwood-dominated stands. About 60 percent of the stands with cedar are included in this category. In the boreal forest, cedar is often present around lakes because of the protection against forest fires and its capacity to resist the mechanical effect of ice (33).

In the Northeastern United States

Cedar is found on a wide range of sites and in a diversity of forest types in the northeastern United States. It occurs most often in mixed-species stands with balsam fir and red spruce, and with northern hardwoods. Though often regarded as a minor species, the density and volume of cedar are substantial, particularly in Maine where it is most abundant (Fig. 4).

U.S. Forest Service Forest Inventory and Analysis (FIA) data indicate that there are more than 1 billion cedar growing-stock trees (diameter at breast height [d.b.h.] ≥12.7 cm [5.0 in]) in New York, Vermont, New Hampshire, and Maine. Eighty-three percent of these trees are in Maine, 10 percent are in New York, 7 percent are in Vermont, and less than 1 percent are in New Hampshire. These trees represent more than 560 million m³ (2 billion ft³) of volume.

The most common forest-type group in the Northeast is maple/beech/yellow birch (forest-type groups and types are those used by FIA [6]). Though 10 percent of the cedar growing-stock trees in the region are in this forest-type group, this species represents less than 1 percent of the stems and volume. Nevertheless, this amounts to more than 100 million stems and 7 million m³ (260 million ft³) of volume.

Seventy-seven percent of the cedar growing-stock trees in the Northeast are in the spruce/fir forest-type group (this includes the cedar, balsam fir, red spruce, red spruce/balsam fir, and black spruce forest types). In the northern white-cedar forest type, cedar represents 34 percent (almost 500 million) of the stems and 58 percent (34 million m³ [1.2 billion ft³]) of the volume (second only to balsam fir). Cedar accounts for 2 to 3 percent of the stems and 5 to 10 percent of the volume in the remaining forest types in the spruce/fir forest-type group; of these, it is most abundant in the balsam fir and red spruce/balsam fir types.

There are almost 0.5 million hectares (1.2 million acres) of northern white-cedar forest type in the region; more than 400,000 hectares (1 million acres, or 88 percent) are in Maine. Seventy-five percent of the area in the northern white-cedar forest type is on lowlands: 54 percent are on flatwoods and 21 percent are on swamp and bogs. Remaining acres of the northern white-cedar forest type are on uplands: almost 20 percent are on rolling uplands and 2 percent are on moist slopes and coves. The majority of these forests are on mesic soils, though swamps and bogs are hydric.

In Ontario

As in other jurisdictions, cedar in Ontario is found in pure and mixed stands with its abundance reflecting parent stock abundance, soil, climate, and past disturbances (Fig. 6). Stands with cedar cover over 3.8 million hectares (9.4 million acres) while stands that are dominated by cedar cover 0.8 million hectares (1.9 million acres) within the zone where commercial forestry can occur (138). The volume of cedar within

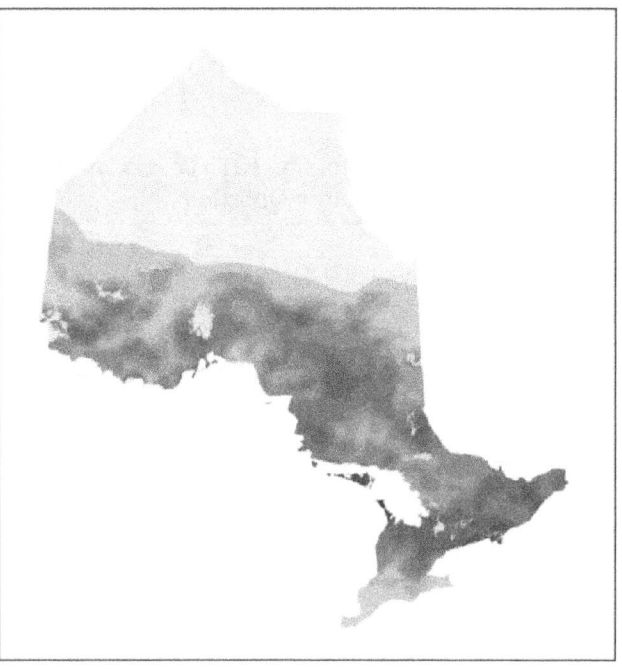

Figure 6.—Distribution and abundance of cedar in Ontario. Darker color indicates a higher abundance of cedar (138). Reproduced with the permission of Larry Watkins, OMNR [138].

the zone where commercial forestry can occur is 133 million m³ (4.7 billion ft³) representing about 2.8 percent of the growing stock in the province.

The most recent summary of forest resources in the province (138) shows cedar is often associated with black spruce, white birch, aspen, and balsam fir. Cedar is most abundant in the Lowland Conifer provincial forest type followed by the Upland Conifer and Mixed-wood forest types (Table 6). Cedar is often found in high abundance on organic soils and on soils that have moist to wet moisture regimes with moderate to high soil fertility in central Ontario (103). In northwestern Ontario it occurs under similar conditions plus rich and dry conditions while in northeastern Ontario it occurs in highest abundance on wet sites with moderate fertility (103).

Description of four typical cedar sites

Assessments leading to prescriptions must consider site conditions among other parameters. General conditions for cedar may be summarized in four categories of sites (Appendix II):

- Upland—stands on very thin soil or outcrops
- Upland—stands on dry or well drained deep soils
- Lowland—stands on moist, deep mineral soils
- Lowland—stands on very moist, deep mineral soils or organic soils

The description of these categories provides information about potential production, physical environment, vegetation, and constraints (competition, trafficability, soil fragility, and risk of windthrow). References to and descriptions of other general or regional classifications (North American associations, Quebec's ecological types, or Ontario's ecosites) can be found in Appendix III.

Table 6.—Gross total volume (GTV) of cedar compared to the GTV for all species in all provincial forest types that include cedar in Ontario (138)

Provincial Forest Type	GTV of Cedar (thousand m³)	GTV of Species (thousand m³)	% Cedar
White birch	3,325	353,456	0.94
Conifer lowland	57,018	828,559	6.88
Conifer upland	37,026	1,169,862	3.16
Mixed wood	21,785	886,548	2.46
Jack pine	22	311,521	0.01
Poplar	1,066	601,108	0.18
Red and white pine	2,491	215,419	1.16
Tolerant hardwoods	10,205	481,119	2.12
Total	132,938	4,847,592	2.74

This section discusses the process for developing or adjusting silvicultural prescriptions to manage cedar in a variety of stands. Few studies of cedar silviculture exist compared to other commercially valuable tree species. Therefore, these recommendations are based on life history, stand dynamics, and ecology of the species, coupled with data from the few silvicultural trials that have been conducted throughout its range.

Silvicultural prescriptions for cedar must be based on knowledge of the species' ecological characteristics and commodity and noncommodity potentials. Assessments leading to prescriptions must consider not only cedar, but site and species composition. Often, cedar grows among many other species and is not the main component of the stand. This may mean that the silvicultural treatment (see Appendix IV for treatment descriptions) will be selected based on the requirements of, and management objectives for, species other than cedar. Even in that case, it is desirable to consider whether and how cedar can be maintained and promoted.

The Process of Selecting a Silvicultural Treatment

Information Needs for Silvicultural Assessment

Silvicultural assessment is a diagnostic process that requires careful consideration of multiple types of information. Varying amounts of effort are required to complete this assessment depending on the size of the ownership and the forester's familiarity with the stands to be treated. We identify four categories of information that should be considered when choosing silvicultural systems and prescriptions (Fig. 7).

- **Forest management objectives:** All management objectives—short- and long-term, commodity and noncommodity—should be identified. Wood production, biodiversity maintenance, wildlife habitat management, and recreation opportunities, among others, may be considerations. Because of its ecological values, niche market potential, and common occurrence as a minor species, objectives for cedar may differ from those of other species in a stand. The more precisely the objectives are defined, the more adequate the prescription will be.

- **Characteristics of the stand and site:** There are many parameters to consider. Stand structure and density, tree maturity, species composition, tree quality and vigor, and regeneration status are examples. In the case of cedar, it is important to be able to objectively place cedar into the context of the whole stand, in terms of its abundance and horizontal and vertical distribution. Potentials and limitations related to site characteristics, such as slope, drainage, wind exposure, and soil

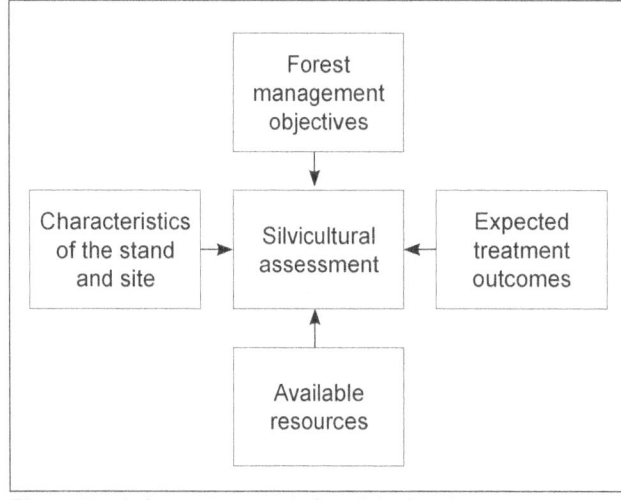

Figure 7.—Information needs for silvicultural assessment (35). Figure by Guy Lessard, CERFO, based on [35], used with permission.

thickness and texture, are important considerations. Reference to the site types described in Appendix II, "Description of four typical cedar sites," of this guide is recommended.

- **Available resources:** Determine the means (human, material, and economic) through which treatments could be applied and the feasibility of treatment application. Managers must consider the qualifications and availability of staff, contractors, and equipment, as well as the potential for commercial harvest or subsidies.

- **Expected treatment outcomes:** Consider the effect of treatments on residual tree growth and stand conditions. Treatments have the potential to affect future product quality and volume, wildlife habitat, aesthetics, recreation, water quality, and nontimber forest products. Possible changes to the site fertility, hydrology, and microclimate should also be considered. Reasonable predictions of wood production can be done using yield statistics (Appendix I).

Steps in Planning and Implementing Silvicultural Treatments

Developing a silvicultural system is a problem-solving process that involves identifying and evaluating multiple options. Appendix V provides a silvicultural assessment form to help gather and analyze data from the field. We outline six steps:

Step 1: Gap analysis between current stand condition and management objectives. Consider current conditions compared to desired future conditions. What is the potential for achieving the management objectives?

Step 2: Identify problems for management. Is there immediate need for action: maturity of trees, sanitation problems, overstocked stand, or need for regeneration? Consider also the relative importance of limiting factors. Sound decisionmaking involves recognizing impediments to success. Are tree species composition, quality, and vigor sufficient for management? If regeneration is desired, will browsing impede recruitment? Are there low expected harvest revenues or market constraints?

Step 3: Identify options. Consider which silvicultural actions are appropriate. For example, is even- or uneven-age silviculture appropriate? If growth improvements are needed, should you selectively remove less desirable species or systematically reduce density? If regeneration is desired but not present, can natural regeneration be achieved or is artificial regeneration required? Consider all management alternatives, including no treatment.

Step 4: Select suitable options and drop the others. Weigh the pros and cons of each option with regard to the objectives and available resources. Considering the anticipated treatment effects on forest resources is essential, as is choosing a silvicultural system.

Step 5: Develop and implement a silvicultural prescription. Identify the treatment and associated details of application that best meet the identified objectives, in light of the constraints of site and resources. In addition, monitoring criteria are developed to allow post-treatment evaluation.

Step 6: Evaluate the results. Adapt future management in light of your successes or failures. For a species such as cedar where basic and applied knowledge is often lacking, this is crucial step of the process.

Considerations for Cedar Silviculture

Reproduction and Early Growth

Cedar reproduces by sexual (seed) and asexual (vegetative) means (29, 71). Layering, the most prevalent form of asexual reproduction, commonly occurs on moist, lowland sites (site types S3 and S4; see Appendix II) (71, 99).

Natural regeneration from seed depends on the proximity of a seed source and the forest floor condition (79). Reported distances for cedar seed dispersal are 45 to 60 m (about 145 to 200 ft) (7, 71). However, these distances will likely be much lower in partial cuts where wind speed is reduced and neighboring trees constitute a physical barrier for seed dispersal (84). For practical purposes, a sufficient seed density is most likely to occur within a distance equivalent to two tree heights.

As with all tree species, genetic diversity should be considered. This issue may be particularly important for cedar because of its occurrence as small isolated and scattered stands or individuals. Further research is needed to determine the minimal cedar density and distribution at the landscape level for maintaining a viable and diverse gene pool. The role of vegetative reproduction in this regard is also unclear. At a minimum, care should be taken to ensure that regeneration is established prior to the removal of mature cedar trees; this will ensure that cedar continues to be present in the stands and protect genetic diversity.

Cedar has relatively stringent requirements for seedbeds. Wet lowland stands (site types S3 and S4) with numerous hummocks support abundant cedar regeneration when a seed source is present; these sites also have less competing understory vegetation (23). Logs and stumps in advanced stages of decay are excellent germination sites because of moisture retention through droughty periods and easy root penetration (22, 27, 28) (Fig. 8). Mat-forming bryophytes on regeneration nurse logs may favor seedling establishment and help prevent seedling desiccation in periods of moisture stress (63). Increasing the number of large logs on the ground may increase cedar abundance relative to balsam fir (128), though an abundance of fresh logging slash can lead to seedling establishment failures (58). Forest managers are encouraged to leave coarse woody material, particularly well decomposed logs, on the forest floor to bolster seedling development.

Abundant cedar regeneration has also been observed on road cuts and prescribed burns where a seed source is available and understory vegetation is sparse; regeneration on leaf litter and thick mosses is limited (28, 117). Mechanical scarification and soil mounding can be used to increase cedar establishment if no advance regeneration is present (73, 79), though care should be taken to protect the root systems of seed trees during scarification. Removing aggressive and deeply rooted competition, such as mountain maple (*Acer spicatum* Lam.) (68), may be an alternative to avoid deep scarification, and can be mechanized or accomplished with herbicides where permitted.

Figure 8.—Cedar regeneration at Sainte-Anne-des-Monts, Quebec. Photo by Stéphane Tremblay, MRNF, used with permission.

Because moisture availability is a critical factor at the germination and early growth stage, partial shade can yield higher germination rates than full sunlight (22, 79). Partial shade can be provided with small gaps (less than one tree height wide) or cuts that remove up to 50 percent of the basal area in stands with basal area around 25 m²/ha (109 ft²/ac) (79). Desiccation of cedar seedlings may occur in full sunlight. The light available to cedar seedlings is dependent on both understory and overstory vegetation, with understory vegetation having a great effect on cedar seedling establishment and recruitment in some stand types (79). Competition can be especially important in upland hardwood or mixed-wood stands growing on dry or deep moist soils (site type S2) or in lowland hardwood or mixed-wood stands on moist deep mineral or organic soils (site type S3).

Though many conditions lead to seedling establishment, cedar is notoriously difficult to grow to the sapling stage. Abundance of cedar seedlings does not guarantee adequate sapling recruitment (58). This species has slower seedling growth than competitors such as balsam fir, shrubs, and associated hardwoods. In addition, cedar is a preferred browse species for deer throughout its range; it is preferred over balsam fir, aspen, and jack pine (*Pinus banksiana* Lamb.) (131-133). In areas with large deer populations, herbivory is often the leading cause of a lack of cedar sapling recruitment because cedar requires at least 20 to 40 years to grow out of deer-browsing height (3 m [10 ft]) (69). It has been observed that cedar seedlings will not maintain growth if more than 25 percent of their foliage is browsed (1). In several experimental trials in areas of high deer-browsing pressure, no cedar seedlings survived outside fenced exclosures after 10 years (31).

Because of slow growth and difficulties with recruitment, advance regeneration of cedar is often imperative to successful regeneration. Regeneration cannot be considered secured until seedlings have grown out of browsing height.² Where several deer yards are present in an area, a forest manager may want to assess the current and desired future deer population, deer yard habitat quality and availability over time, and, if deer yards are not limiting, select one or more yards to intentionally reduce suitability to

---

²In general, deer browse up to a height of 2 m (45). Therefore the minimal tree height should be 3 m to ensure a minimal crown length of 1 m.

Key Points for Successful Cedar Establishment

- Consider deer populations when selecting a cedar regeneration strategy.
- Bolster advance cedar regeneration through partial harvesting.
- Avoid canopy openings wider than one tree height.
- Increase germination success by soil scarification and mounding or by maintaining well decomposed coarse woody material within two tree heights of seed-bearing cedar.
- Reduce competition from faster-growing associates.
- Proceed to planting or direct seeding of cedar on sites without established regeneration or a local seed source.
- When deer browsing pressure is high, saplings must be out of reach (>3 m [10 ft]) before the regeneration can be considered secured.

deer for a couple of decades (e.g., by reducing cover) and work to promote cedar regeneration. Fencing may be required in areas of high deer populations.

Even though a partial canopy can benefit seedling establishment and early growth, it has been reported that heavy overstory shade after seedling establishment results in virtually no seedling survival (31). Cedar existing as advance regeneration shows strong responses to overstory release, even after extended periods of suppression (58, 61); height growth of established seedlings increases proportionally to light availability, with a sixfold increase between a closed canopy and full sunlight (79).

In areas where advance regeneration is not adequate and seed sources are not present, fill- or under-planting can be used. Planted seedlings have shown good survival and growth in gaps measuring about 1.5 tree height (79). Artificial seeding has also been shown to increase seedling establishment on disturbed seedbeds and under partial canopy (79) (refer to Table 4 for seedbed preferences). Vegetation control after planting will likely be required because cedar grows more slowly than many of its competitors. Considerations relative to browsing mentioned for natural regeneration also apply.

Growth of Saplings, Poles, and Larger Trees

Recruitment of cedar into the sapling and merchantable size classes are concerns in several U.S. states and Canada (76, 77). Statistics show that recruitment is low (Appendix I). Recruitment can be improved through early (precommercial) treatments; later (commercial) treatments focus on improving the growth of established stems and decreasing the time needed to reach larger sizes. Without explicit management objectives to retain cedar in mixed-species stands, it is likely that over time the proportion

of cedar will decline relative to associated species with higher growth rates and lower palatability unless cedar is favored through intermediate treatments (69, 77).

Because many cedar trees originate beneath an existing overstory, and overtopped cedar trees respond positively even after extended periods of suppression (62), treatments to release immature stems should have favorable outcomes. Removing competing vegetation (i.e., faster-growing balsam fir and hardwoods) in precommercial thinning and/or cleaning operations is recommended to improve the recruitment of cedar into the merchantable size classes (77). Because this treatment could make cedar more visible or accessible to deer, it could be delayed where the competing vegetation is not too dense until cedar saplings are over 3 m high (10 ft) in areas with high deer densities. When conducting precommercial thinning in favor of other species, cedar can be treated as an "invisible species" and left in place because it will normally occur in low numbers and have little impact on the target species, given its slow growth.

Diameter increment increases with tree size at early stages and levels off progressively afterward (Appendix I, section "Reference Values for Diameter Increment"). The average time of passage (number of years required to grow from one diameter class to

---

- **Seedlings** are young trees having a d.b.h. of no more than 1 cm (⅜ inch) and no more than 1.5 m (5 ft) tall.
- **Saplings** are trees larger then seedlings but with a d.b.h. of no more than 9 cm (3.5 in).
- **Poles** are trees with a d.b.h. greater than 9 cm (3.5 in) but not more than 19 cm (7.5 in).
- **Larger trees** have a d.b.h. of more than 19 cm (7.5 in).

the next) varies from 7 to 27 years for 2-cm diameter classes and 9 to 31 years for 1-inch classes (Appendix I, section "Reference Values for Diameter Increment"). Promotion from one size class to another can be estimated with transition probabilities, which were calculated for 20-year periods, by combining diameter growth and tree mortality (Appendix I, section "Stand Dynamics").

Response of cedar to commercial thinning has been poorly documented. An unreplicated trial shows that lowland cedar stands can have a measurable growth response (116), and suggests that thinning should focus on better-drained swamps because stands on poor sites with stagnant water may show little response to thinning. However, up to now there is little empirical evidence of this. Another thinning experiment (41) on a "fertile swamp" showed that cedar growth was not affected by a second thinning over a large range of densities. Regardless of the species mixture or treatment, intermediate treatments should focus on retaining sound individuals (i.e., free from decay) when possible. It should be noted, however, that presence of butt rot does not reduce the value of trees for shingle production.

In the absence of a proven thinning method, we make the following recommendations based on experience with other conifers and preliminary data:

(a) Thinning should be considered when trees are overtopped or experiencing side shade if the crown length is greater than 33 percent (trees with smaller live crowns lack vigor and may not respond to release). To favor the long-term development of dominant or codominant crown classes, crown thinning is recommended over thinning from below. Due to cedar's ability to persist in shaded environments, capturing mortality through low thinning is likely not a priority.

(b) Release cedar in the intermediate and suppressed crown classes because of its capacity to respond even after a long period of suppression.

A forester planning intermediate treatments for cedar should be patient due to its relatively slow growth, long life span, and good response to release (62). It may be necessary to consider a long-term objective for cedar that requires more than one rotation of the companion species.

Key Points about Growth of Saplings, Poles, and Larger Trees

- Cedar recruitment is problematic and warrants attention through intermediate treatments.
- Cedar responds well to release, even after extended periods of suppression.
- Consider treating cedar as an "invisible species" during thinning operations on sites where it is rare.
- In lowlands, cedar growth response to intermediate treatments may be better on sites with moving groundwater.
- When possible, efforts should be made to favor sound trees in a range of canopy positions.
- Windthrow is a concern when thinned to low densities, especially on wet or shallow soils.
- Protect residual cedar trees from damage during all harvesting operations.
- Depending on the crown class of the merchantable cedar trees, crown thinning or improvement cutting should be considered.
- Thinning is not recommended for trees with less than 33 percent or over 50 percent of crown length.

Cedar is well adapted to the stratified canopy and age diversity of uneven-age stands due to its longevity and response to repeated releases even at old ages (62). However, it has the weakest wood of all commercial tree species in North America (7). Careful logging must occur to avoid residual stand damage; operations on wet soils (site type S4) should be conducted during dry or frozen periods of the year to avoid excessive soil compaction, rutting, root damage, and windthrow.

A Decision Guide for Cedar Silviculture

This section offers a decision guide to help forest managers choose the appropriate silvicultural treatment for cedar, with regard to forest management objectives, risk of deer browsing, and cedar silvics. This guide applies to stands or micro-stands, i.e., portions of the main stand where cedar is present. It should supplement, but not replace, your own assessment of objectives and potentials, as proposed in section "The Process of Selecting a Silvicultural Treatment".

Because of the scarcity of knowledge based on operational experience about cedar silviculture, the decision guide is based on existing literature and a limited number of field trials. These recommendations require field validation, as recommended in section "The Process of Selecting a Silvicultural Treatment".

This decision guide was designed considering management goals of (a) ensuring long-term cedar sustainability and (b) producing large-size, high-quality cedar logs (diameter larger than 30 cm [12 in]). Risk of deer browsing is a key decision factor.

Existing silvicultural guides for cedar generally focus on pure stands (70, 83, 92, 122). However, cedar is often found in mixtures with other species, forming a minor component of the forest stand. In such stands, the challenge is to harmonize cedar silviculture with the rest of the stand. Decisions about cedar silviculture need to take into account the silvicultural system and treatments applied to the major component of the stand.

One practical way to do this is to adopt a multiple-treatment approach, where clumps of cedar are treated as micro-stands within the overall matrix (Fig. 9). Silviculture decisions are then made for each micro-stand on an area of about 400 m² (0.1 ac), which corresponds to what can be visually assessed in the field. Similar micro-stands form a silviculture micro-type, which is associated with a single prescription. Such an approach is compatible with the multiple treatment method, a flexible operational system developed for complex stands (89). When cedar is the main species and stands are more homogenous, the process could be applied at the stand scale rather than at the micro-stand.

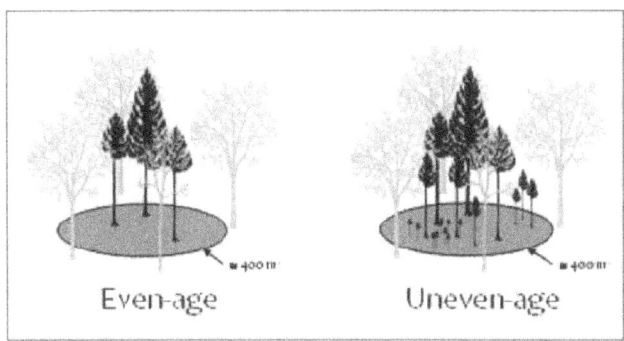

Figure 9.—Schematic views of even-age and uneven-age cedar micro-stands within an even-age hardwood stand. Figure by Guy Lessard, CERFO.

This guide focuses on a limited number of typical stand conditions because all possible cases that can be found in the forest cannot be covered. Our objective is to provide recommendations, and their rationale, for common conditions so that the forester can adapt these to other conditions not specifically addressed by the guide. Figure 10 is a decision key to help forest managers choose the most appropriate management regime for a given situation.

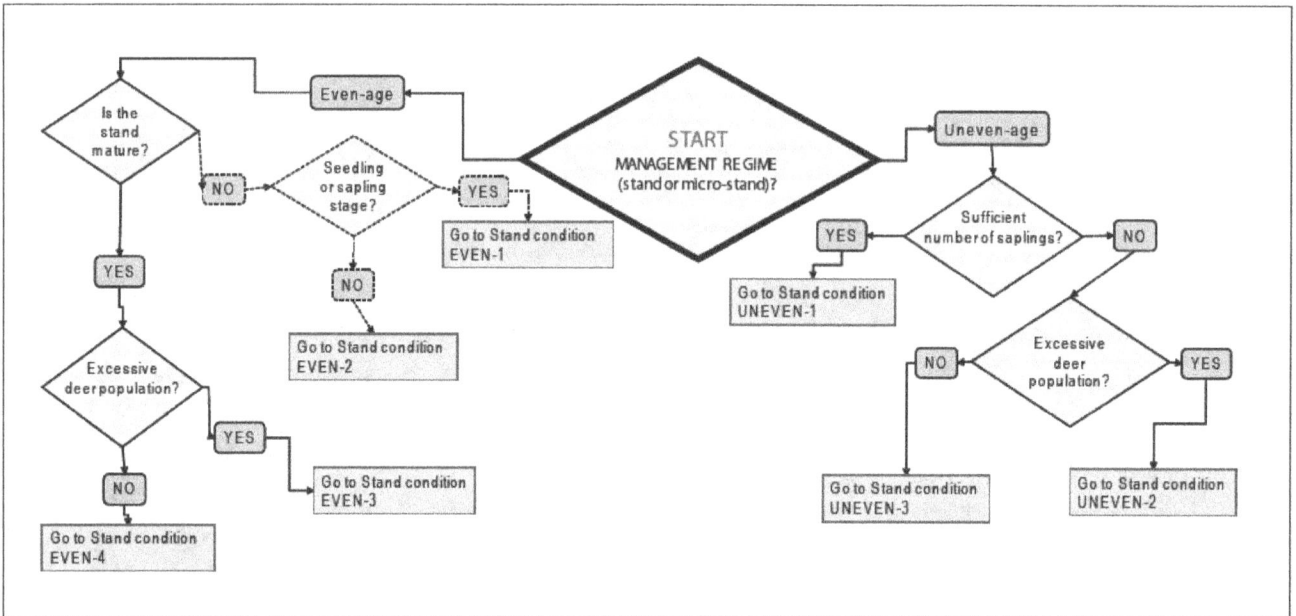

Figure 10.—Decision key for cedar management. Figure by Jean-Claude Ruel, Jean-Martin Lussier, and Guy Lessard for the first version, used with permission.

EVEN-1

Even-age stands/micro-stands in the seedling or sapling stage

- If stand/micro-stand is dense and funds are available, consider precommercial thinning. A good response can be expected, even after long periods of suppression.

Note:

- Precommercial thinning could make cedar saplings more visible to deer and increase browsing; treatment in areas of high deer density should be delayed until the trees are more than 3 m (10 ft) tall.

- When precommercial thinning is conducted in a stand where there is no specific production objective for cedar, cedar can be considered an "invisible species" and left uncut, because it will not compromise the production of most target species.

- Although variations in growth response in relation to site condition can be expected, especially on "extreme" sites (dry upland sites [site type S1] or lowland sites with no ground water circulation [subgroup of site type S4]), there are few data to support this assumption.

EVEN-2

Even-age stands/micro-stands at the pole stage

- Commercial thinning can be considered if stand/micro-stand density is high; thinning should be considered when crown length is between 33 and 50 percent.

- Though few cedar commercial thinning trials have been conducted, cedar trees respond well to release in partially cut stands (76), even at advanced ages (62).

- Reducing canopy closure through thinning may decrease deer yard benefits; deer in northern regions seek deer yards for reduced snow depth, warmer temperatures, lower wind speeds, and greater browse abundance (119).

- Thinnings can be successful in cedar deer yards but overstory density must be sufficient to maintain the canopy closure level prescribed in habitat management guidelines for your region.

- Improvement cutting can be considered if there is a large number of less desirable trees, but windthrow hazard should be considered.

Note:

- To prevent windthrow losses, commercial thinning is not recommended less than 1.5 tree heights from large openings (e.g., clearcuts, roads, etc.).

- Although variations in growth response in relation to site condition can be expected, especially on "extreme sites" (dry upland sites [site type S1] or lowland sites with no ground water circulation [subgroup of site type S4]), there are few data to support this assumption. Therefore, widespread thinning on extreme sites should be avoided until growth responses can be quantified.

EVEN-3

Mature even-age stands/micro-stands in a high deer population area

With an adequate sapling bank

- A shelterwood cut could be used to increase sapling growth while controlling shade-intolerant species. Final overstory removal could be done when a sufficient number of saplings have grown out of reach of deer.

- Overstory removal (see Appendix IV, clearcutting definition) can be used. Given its slow growth rate and the potential for recruitment failures, cedar retention is recommended to ensure a future seed source.

- Deer browsing will likely be a problem as long as saplings remain within the reach of deer

Without an adequate sapling bank

- Because browsing pressure is high, cedar regeneration will be extremely difficult to secure, unless fencing can be used.

- If fencing is used, refer to EVEN-4

(continued on next page)

EVEN-3 (continued)

Mature even-age stands/micro-stands in a high deer population area

Note:

- Saplings are considered in a better position to cope with moisture stresses than seedlings.

- Deer density greater than 4 to 7 deer/km^2 (10-18 deer/mi^2) has a significant impact on forest regeneration. In the field, deer pressure can be assessed with a browsing index, obtained by counting the number of browsed and unbrowsed terminal twigs located 30 to 200 cm (12-79 in) above the ground on 12 to 20 sugar maple saplings growing in stands where cedar is also present (45, 117). The index is equal to the number of browsed shoots divided by the total number of counted shoots. Index values greater than 40 to 50 percent indicate high deer density.

- When browsing pressure is high, the height threshold for well established regeneration should be 3 m (10 ft).

- For even-age stands, the number of saplings required to replace the mature trees depends on stand productivity and target d.b.h. (see Appendix I). It is also a function of the overall density-control strategy, including the number and type of scheduled thinnings.

- Browsing pressure can be controlled with fencing. However, the cost of fencing is usually prohibitive (30). Even though the cost for installing electrical fences can be lower, their maintenance cost is higher compared to conventional fences (30).

- Micro-stands of immature cedar in a mature stand of a shorter-lived species could be retained for a second rotation after overstory removal; however, attention should be paid to leave a sufficient buffer of standing trees (approximately 1.5 tree heights) around the micro-stands to prevent windthrow.

- In stands where cedar trees represent a minor component of a species mixture and will be under-utilized if harvested (e.g., consolidated with other species for chipping), cedar, particularly those of small size (i.e., poletimber) should be retained following overstory removal as growing stock and seed source, even if isolated. The potential ecological and economic benefits of these reserves likely outweigh the risk of mortality in this situation.

- Competition by shrubs or faster growing tree species is to be expected on certain sites; this competition is generally less on lowland on very moist soil and upland on very thin soil than upland on dry to fresh soil and lowland on moist soil.

EVEN-4

Mature even-age stands/micro-stands in a low deer population area

With an adequate seedling bank

- Overstory removal (see Appendix IV for clearcutting definition) can be used but seedlings are likely to experience moisture stress unless they are well established (30 cm [1 ft] tall).

- A partial overstory removal could be used to increase seedling and sapling growth while controlling shade-intolerant species. For seedlings shorter than 30 cm (1 ft), a residual basal over 13 m^2/ha (57 ft^2/ac) is recommended.

(continued on next page)

EVEN-4 (continued)

Mature even-age stands/micro-stands in a low deer population area

With a closed canopy and without an adequate seedling bank

- Clearcutting is likely to lead to a failure of cedar regeneration because of lack of seed source and dry seedbed conditions.

- The seed tree system is likely to fail due to a limited seed supply and seedbed moisture stresses, as well as windthrow of isolated trees on lowland sites. Retention of clumps where there is cedar may be an option to help establish new regeneration.

- Uniform shelterwood, retaining a crown closure of at least 60 percent (103) or a basal area of at least 13 m²/ha (57 ft²/ac) to reduce moisture stress, combined with scarification could lead to good seedling establishment; extended time between entries would be beneficial for cedar. It is suggested that cedar stands are not "established" until new seedlings have reached 30 cm (1 ft) in height even when browsing pressure is low. This may take 6 to 13 years after the regeneration harvest, even with good seedling stocking (58, 76).

- Although planting cedar may be an option for regenerating stands without an adequate seedling bank, no guidance is currently available from the literature. Creating canopy gaps (625 m² [0.15 ac]) and planting cedar within has given good initial results both in terms of survival and growth. Planting cedar under a partial canopy leads to good survival but growth is reduced.

With an open canopy, and without an adequate seedling bank

- Clearcutting is likely to lead to a failure of cedar regeneration because of lack of seed source and dry seedbed conditions.

- Partial cuts are not required because the canopy is already open. Patch scarification could be used to induce the establishment of a new cohort of seedlings if shrub density is low (see note below on patch scarification); planting could also be used.

- Brushing should be used to reduce shrub cover in combination with scarification in cases of high brush cover.

Note:

- Brushing can be done locally around scarified patches.

- Competition after overstory removal can be high (79).

- To prevent windthrow losses, shelterwood is not recommended within 1.5 tree heights from large openings (e.g., clearcuts, roads, etc.).

- In stands where cedar trees represent a minor component of a species mixture and will be under-utilized if harvested (e.g., consolidated with other species for chipping), cedar, particularly those of small size (i.e., pole) should be retained following overstory removal as growing stock and seed source, even if isolated. The potential ecological and economic benefits of these reserves likely outweigh the risk of mortality in this situation.

- To provide sufficient seed, scarification should be done within a distance to seed trees equal to no more than twice their height.

- Large dead woody debris on the ground and decaying stumps should be protected during scarification, because they are prime sites for cedar regeneration.

UNEVEN-1

Uneven-age stands with an adequate sapling bank

- Single-tree selection can be used to keep moisture levels high and ground temperatures low (71, 76).
- Group selection or patch-selection[3] with canopy openings greater than two tree heights can be used in stands with a large component of saplings that can better cope with moisture stress than seedlings. Guidelines to manage the size and number of gaps per cutting cycle for a patch-selection system are available (101).
- Irregular shelterwood, with retention of cedar after the overstory removal, can also be used when obtaining a sustained yield at the stand level or maintaining a permanent canopy are not required by regulation or management objectives.

Note:

- Managing cedar micro-stands as uneven-age patches is simpler when the whole stand is managed as uneven-age.
- Extra care to residual trees must be given, to avoid fungal infection and decay due to wounds caused by scarification or harvest. Winter harvest is the preferred option.
- Area-based regeneration methods such as group selection, create adjacent patches of overstory and regenerating vegetation that may attract deer and other mammals (20). If this system is used, moose and deer populations must be low or controlled with fences.

[3]Generally, in group selection, the harvest is managed in terms of number of adjacent trees to be removed (with a gap size smaller than two tree heights), rather than in terms of a fixed-gap size. In this case, we should refer to patch selection (101).

UNEVEN-2

Uneven-age stands with a high deer population, without an adequate sapling bank

- Fencing could be used in combination with selection cutting, especially if group selection is used (see note). Ideally the canopy openings should be less than one tree height in diameter to induce seedling establishment. If fencing is used, refer to UNEVEN-3;
- Without fencing, selection cutting could still be used to take advantage of existing poles. A lack of cedar recruitment is likely to occur, making this approach unsustainable over the long term.

Note:

- Deer density over 4 to 7 deer/km^2 (10-18 deer/mi^2) has a significant impact on forest regeneration. See the browsing index in the EVEN-3 section.
- Group selection or similar area-based regeneration methods create adjacent patches of overstory and regenerating vegetation that may attract ungulates (20). If this system is used, deer may need to be controlled with fences. However, the cost of fencing is usually prohibitive (30). Even though the cost for installing electrical fences can be lower, their maintenance cost is higher compared to conventional fences.
- Managing cedar micro-stands as uneven-age is simpler when the whole stand is managed as uneven-age.
- Extra care must be given to residual trees to avoid fungal infection and decay due to wounds caused by scarification or harvest.

UNEVEN-3

Uneven-age stands in a low deer population area, without an adequate seedling bank

With a closed tree canopy

- Irregular shelterwood or group selection cutting, with retention of cedar, can be used in combination with patch scarification. Additional fill-planting in gaps could be used if sufficient seed trees are not present.

With an open canopy (crown closure below 60 percent) but a dense understory

- Use vegetation management to remove or control understory competing vegetation and patch scarification because light transmission through the canopy is already sufficient for seedling establishment. Additional fill- or under-planting could be used. Follow-up vegetation management will be required.

With an open canopy but without a dense understory

- Patch scarification can be used to enhance seedling establishment close to seed trees or if direct seeding is used.
- Fill- or under-planting could be used.

Note:

- Managing cedar micro-stands as uneven-age patches is simpler when the whole stand is managed as uneven-age.
- Extra care must be given to residual trees to avoid fungal infection and decay due to wounds caused by scarification or harvest.

Ecological Silviculture

Silviculture is applied to control the composition, structure, and quality of residual stands. As such, it can be used to create desired conditions for any objective, both commodity and noncommodity. In traditional practice, silviculture is used to ensure that forests produce a defined and continuous supply of timber. Yet many landowners desire, or are mandated, to maintain the ecological integrity of their forests. Simply applying conventional silvicultural systems may not meet this additional objective.

Ecological forestry uses knowledge of natural disturbance regimes and ecological processes to make management decisions about the type, intensity, and frequency of silvicultural treatments, and thus the resulting stand structure and composition (127).

Forest managers need to compare silvicultural systems and natural disturbances to identify the differences between these types of disturbances. Traditionally managed uneven-age stands, for example, are often characterized by a regularity of disturbance and homogeneity of horizontal structure and composition atypical of multi-age stands resulting from natural gap dynamics (126). Similarly, even-age treatments that remove the overstory, such as the clearcut or uniform shelterwood methods, create simpler stand structures with fewer or no residual trees and less dead wood than stand-replacing natural disturbances (43), e.g., spruce budworm (*Choristoneura fumiferana* [Clem.]) and fire.

In ecological forestry, consideration of the disturbance type and rate should serve as guides for the type, intensity, and frequency of silvicultural treatments applied. Modifications of treatments to maintain biological legacies via permanent retention, or create spatial heterogeneity of composition or structure, are often warranted. Such modifications may require that some commodity-production objectives, such as stem quality improvement, are sacrificed or less fully attained.

Area-based silvicultural methods, such as group or patch selection and group shelterwood, have been suggested for ecological forestry in the northeastern United States and adjacent areas of Canada (125). These approaches offer a means of directly controlling canopy disturbance rates and may be effectively used to emulate natural disturbances. In ecosystems or on sites where stand-replacing disturbances predominate, the observed spatial extent and range of return intervals of naturally occurring disturbances serve as potential models for the rotations and sizes of even-age stands (130). Similarly, where the natural disturbance regime is characterized by canopy gaps, their frequency and extent may serve as guides for cutting cycles and sizes of openings in uneven-age stands.

Because natural disturbances rarely result in complete mortality of standing trees, retention of some minimum number of residual trees is likely to be an important component of ecological forestry. Cedar's longevity, ability to respond well to release even at advanced ages, and many biodiversity values make it an excellent legacy or retention tree. This approach has the added benefit of retaining cedar seed sources, which may prove desirable should a regeneration failure occur.

Managing under a natural disturbance paradigm requires foresters to familiarize themselves not only with the silvics of their species, but also with the disturbance ecology of the region (127). Because cedar is commonly found as a component of mixed-species stands, we have recommended a micro-stand approach to assessment and treatment. Such an approach is well suited to adaptation of silvicultural systems for maintenance of ecological integrity in our region, where the forest as a whole, and the majority of stands, are naturally heterogeneous.

The authors would like to thank those who provided feedback on an earlier version of this document at a session in Maine: Ked Coffin, the late Stephen Coleman, Mike Dann, Marc Deschene, Dave Dow, Kenny Fergusson, Roger Greene, Jacob Guimond, Michael Jurgiewich, Vernon Kelly, Vernon Labbe, Jim O'Malley, Jay Plourde, Jerry Poulin, Dan Smith, Matt Stedman, the late Hugh Violette, Chris White, and Ken White.

We are also grateful to the people from Quebec who provided us with new ideas and information following the review of the document: Annie Malenfant, Michel Huot, Patrick Lupien, Barbara Hébert, Daniel Kneeshaw, Philippe Meek, Jean-Claude Racine, Luc Mageau, Anouk Pohu, and Daniel Pin.

Our draft manuscript was reviewed by Yves Bergeron, Mike Brienesse, Johann Housset, and Robert Seymour. We gratefully acknowledge their constructive comments and contributions.

We thank George McCaskill of the U.S. Forest Service, Forest Inventory and Analysis, for providing us with data about amount of cedar and its forest-type associations in the northeastern United States.

Special thanks to Charles Tardif (Vice President Corporate Development and Procurement) and François Nobert (Wood Procurement Manager) from Maibec Inc. for their contributions to this project.

When you know:	Multiply by:	To find:
Millimeters (mm)	0.0394	Inches (in)
Centimeters (cm)	0.394	Inches (in)
Meters (m)	3.28	Feet (ft)
Meters (m)	1.094	Yards (yd)
Kilometers (km)	0.621	Miles (mi)
Hectares (ha)	2.47	Acres (ac)
Square meters (m^2)	10.76	Square feet (ft^2)
Cubic decimeters (dm^3)	0.0353	Cubic feet (ft^3)
Square kilometers (km^2)	0.386	Square miles (mi^2)
Cubic meters (m^3)	35.3	Cubic feet (ft^3)
Cubic meters apparent (m^3)	3.62	Cords
Cubic meters solid (m^3)	2.41	Cords
Square meters per hectare (m^2/ha)	4.37	Square feet per acre (ft^2/ac)
Cubic meters per hectare (m^3/ha)	14.29	Cubic feet per acre (ft^3/ac)
Trees per hectare	0.405	Trees per acre
Degrees Celsius (°C)	$1.8\,°C + 32$	Degrees Fahrenheit (°F)

1. Aldous, S.E. 1941. **Deer management suggestions for northern white cedar types.** Journal of Wildlife Management. 5(1): 90-94.

2. Archambault, S.; Bergeron, Y. 1992. **An 802-year tree-ring chronology from the Quebec boreal forest.** Canadian Journal of Forest Research. 22: 674-682.

3. Banton, E.; Johnson, J.; Lee, H.; Racey, G.; Uhlig, P.; Wester, M. 2009. **Ecosites of Ontario. Version 2.0.** Sault Ste. Marie, ON: Ontario Ministry of Natural Resources. 91 p.

4. Basham, J.T. 1991. **Stem decay in living trees in Ontario's forests: a user's compendium and guide.** Inf. Rep. O-X-408. Sault Ste. Marie, ON: Forestry Canada, Ontario Region, Great Lakes Forestry Center. 69 p.

5. Baumflek, M.J.; Emery, M.R.; Ginger, C. 2010. **Culturally and economically important nontimber forest product of northern Maine.** Gen. Tech. Rep. NRS-68. Newtown Square, PA: U.S. Department of Agriculture, Forest Service, Northern Research Station. 74 p.

6. Bechtold, W.A.; Patterson, P.L., eds. 2005. **The enhanced forest inventory and analysis program: national sampling design and estimation procedures.** Asheville, NC: U.S. Department of Agriculture, Forest Service, Southern Research Station. 85 p.

7. Behr, E.A. 1974. **Distinguishing heartwood in northern white cedar.** Wood Science. 6(4): 394-395.

8. Behr, E.A. 1976. **Special physical and chemical properties of northern white cedar.** In: National northern white cedar conference; 1976 February; East Lansing, MI. Publ. 3-76. East Lansing, MI: Michigan State University: 11-15.

9. Bergeron, Y. 2000. **Species and stand dynamics in the mixed woods of Quebec's southern boreal forest.** Ecology. 81: 1500-1516.

10. Berven, K. 2011. **U.S. Forest Service northern conifer experimental forest: historical review and examples of silvicultural research applications.** Orono, ME: University of Maine. 115 p. M.S. thesis.

11. Biggar, H.P. 1924. **The voyages of Jacques Cartier.** Ottawa, ON: Public Archives of Canada. 330 p.

12. Blum, B.M. 1990. *Picea rubens* **Sarg. - red spruce.** In: Burns, R.M.; Honkala, B.H., eds. Silvics of North America. Vol. 1. Agric. Hndbk. 654. Washington, DC: U.S. Department of Agriculture, Forest Service: 250-259.

13. Boucher, Y.; Arseneault, D.; Sirois, L. 2006. **Logging-induced change (1930-2002) of a preindustrial landscape at the northern range limit of northern hardwoods, eastern Canada.** Canadian Journal of Forest Research. 36: 505-517.

14. Boulet, B. 2003. **Les champignons des arbres de l'est de l'Amérique du Nord.** Québec, QC: Les Publications du Québec. 727 p.

15. Boulet, B. 2007. **Défauts et indices de la carie des arbres.** 2e édition. Québec, QC: Les Publications du Québec. 317 p.

16. Bowyer, J.L.; Shmulsky, R.; Havgreen, J.G. 2005. **Le bois et ses usages.** Montréal, QC: Centre collégial de développement de matériel didactique. 528 p.

17. Bryan, R.R. 2007. **Focus Species Forestry: A guide to integrating timber and biodiversity management in Maine.** Third Edition. Falmouth, ME: Maine Audubon. 92 p.

18. Buongiorno, J.; Gilless, J.K. 2003. **Decision methods forest resource management.** Burlington, MA: Academic Press. 439 p.

19. Canadian Council of Forest Ministers. 2010. **National forestry database.** Ottawa, ON: Canadian Council of Forest Ministers. Available at http://nfdp.ccfm.org/terms/terms_e.php. (Accessed December 2, 2010).

20. Castleberry, S.B.; Ford, W.M.; Miller, K.V.; Smith, W.P. 2000. **Influences of herbivory and canopy openings in size on forest regeneration in a southern bottomland hardwood forest.** Forest Ecology and Management. 131: 57-64.

21. Cauboue, M. 2007. **Description écologique des forêts du Québec.** Montréal, QC: Centre collégial de développement de matériel didactique. 294 p.

22. Caulkins, H.L., Jr. 1967. **The ecology and reproduction of northern white cedar.** Ann Arbor, MI: University of Michigan. 70 p. M.S. thesis.

23. Chimner, R.A.; Hart, J.B. 1996. **Hydrology and microtopography effects on northern white-cedar regeneration in Michigan's Upper Peninsula.** Canadian Journal of Forest Research. 26(3): 389-393.

24. Corbet, D.; McCaul, E. 2010. **Cedar pilot project report one: Preliminary data summary and project description.** Peterborough, ON: Northwest Science and Information, Government of Ontario. 27 p.

25. Cornett, M.W.; Frelich, L.E.; Puettmann, K.J.; Reich, P.B. 2000. **Conservation implications of browsing by *Odocoileus virginianus* in remanant upland *Thuja occidentalis* forests.** Biological Conservation. 93: 359-369.

26. Cornett, M.W.; Puettmann, K.J.; Frelich, L.E.; Reich, P.B. 2001. **Comparing the importance of seedbed and canopy type in the restoration of upland *Thuja occidentalis* forests in northeastern Minnesota.** Restoration Ecology. 9(4): 386-396.

27. Cornett, M.W.; Reich, P.B.; Puettmann, K.J. 1997. **Canopy feedbacks and microtopography regulate conifer seeding distribution in two Minnesota conifer-deciduous forests.** Ecoscience. 4(3): 353-364.

28. Cornett, M.W.; Reich, P.B.; Puettmann, K.J.; Frelich, L.E. 2000. **Seedbed and moisture availability determine safe sites for early *Thuja occidentalis* (Cupressaceae) regeneration.** American Journal of Botany. 87: 1807-1814.

29. Curtis, J.D. 1941. **Report of northern white cedar research in Maine.** Orono, ME: Unpublished manuscript. 23 p. On file at University of Maine, Orono, ME.

30. Cusson, M. 2004. **Le cerf de Virginie: Comment faire face aux dommages qu'il peut causer dans la région de la Chaudière-Appalaches.** Québec, QC: Ministère des Ressources naturelles, de la Faune et des Parcs, Gouvernement du Québec. 13 p.

31. Davis, M.A.; Wrage, K.J.; Reich, P.B. 1998. **Competition between tree seedlings and herbaceous vegetation: support for a theory of resource supply and demand.** Journal of Ecology. 86: 652-661.

32. De Geus, R. 2011. **Personal communication.** Vermont Department of Forests, Parks & Recreation. 112 State St., Montpelier, VT.

33. Denneler, B.; Asselin, H.; Bergeron, Y.; Bégin, Y. 2008. **Decreased fire frequency and increased water levels affect riparian forest dynamics in Southwestern boreal Quebec, Canada.** Canadian Journal of Forest Research. 38: 1083-1094.

34. Déry, S.; Labbé, P. 2006. **Lignes directrices rattachées à l'objectif sur la conservation du bois mort dans les forêts aménagées: sélection de lisières boisées riveraines à soustraire de l'aménagement forestier.** Québec, QC: Gouvernement du Québec, Ministère des Ressources naturelles et de la Faune, Direction de l'environnement forestier. 15 p.

35. Doucet, R.; Pineau, M.; Ruel, J.-C.; Sheedy, G. 1996. **Manuel de foresterie.** Québec, QC: Les Presses de l'Université Laval. 1428 p.

36. Dumais, D.; Prévost, M. 2007. **Management for red spruce conservation in Quebec: the importance of some physiological and ecological characteristics - a review.** Forestry Chronicle. 83(3): 378-392.

37. Durzan, D.J. 2009. **Arginine, scurvy, and Jacques Cartier's "tree of life".** Journal of Ethnobiology & Ethnomedicine. 5: 5.

38. Erdmann, G.G. 1990. *Betula alleghaniensis* **Britton - yellow birch.** In: Burns, R.M.; Honkala, B.H., eds. Silvics of North America. Vol. 2. Agric. Hndbk. 654. Washington, DC: U.S. Department of Agriculture, Forest Service: 133-147.

39. Erichsen-Brown, C. 1989. **Medicinal and other uses of North American plants: an historical survey with special reference to the eastern Indian tribes.** Mineola, NY: Dover Publications. 512 p.

40. Farrar, J.L. 1996. **Les arbres du Canada (Trees in Canada).** St-Laurent, QC: Fides et Service canadien des forêts en collaboration avec Approvisionnements et Services Canada. 502 p.

41. Foltz, J.L.; Knight, F.B.; Allen, D.C.; Mattson, W.J., Jr. 1968. **A technique for sampling populations of the jack-pine budworm.** Forest Science. 14: 277-281.

42. Frank, R.M. 1990. *Abies balsamea* **(L.) Mill. - balsam fir.** In: Burns, R.M.; Honkala, B.H., eds. Silvics of North America. Vol. 1. Agric. Hndbk. 654. Washington, DC: U.S. Department of Agriculture, Forest Service: 26-35.

43. Franklin, J.F.; Berg, D.R.; Thornburgh, D.A.; Tappeiner, J.C. 1997. **Alternative silvicultural approaches to timber harvesting: variable retention harvest systems.** In: Kohm, K.A.; Franklin, J.F., eds. 1997. Creating a forestry for the 21st century: The science of ecosystem management. Washington, DC: Island Press: 111-140.

44. Fraver, S.; White, A.S.; Seymour, R.S. 2009. **Natural disturbance in an old-growth landscape in northern Maine.** Journal of Ecology. 97: 289-298.

45. Frelich, L.E.; Lorimer, C.G. 1985. **Current and predicted long-term effects of deer browsing in hemlock forests in Michigan, USA.** Biological Conservation. 34: 99-120.

46. Frelich, L.E.; Reich, P.B. 1998. **Disturbance severity and threshold responses in the boreal forest.** Conservation Ecology. 2(2): 7.

47. Garber, S.M.; Brown, J.P.; Wilson, D.S.; Maguire, D.A.; Heath, L.S. 2005. **Snag longevity under alternative silvicultural regimes in mixed-species forests of central Maine.** Canadian Journal of Forest Research. 35(4): 787-796.

48. Gashwiler, J.S. 1967. **Conifer seed survival in a western Oregon clearout.** Ecology. 48: 431-438.

49. Godman, R.M.; Lancaster, K. 1990. *Tsuga canadensis* **(L.) Carr - eastern hemlock.** In: Burns, R M ; Honkala, B.H., eds. Silvics of North America. Vol. 1. Agric. Hndbk. 654. Washington, DC: U.S. Department of Agriculture, Forest Service: 604-612.

50. Godman, R.M.; Mattson, G.A. 1976. **Seed crops and regeneration problems of 19 species in northeastern Wisconsin.** Res. Pap. NC-123. St. Paul, MN: U.S. Department of Agriculture, Forest Service, North Central Forest Experiment Station. 5 p.

51. Godman, R.M.; Yawney, H.M.; Tubbs, C.H. 1990. *Acer saccharum* **Marsh. - sugar maple.** In: Burns, R.M.; Honkala, B.H., eds. Silvics of North America. Vol. 2. Agric. Hndbk. 654. Washington, DC: U.S. Department of Agriculture, Forest Service: 78-91.

52. Gosselin, J.; Grondin, P.; Saucier, J.-P. 1998. **Rapport de classification écologique du sous-domaine bioclimatique de l'érablière à bouleau jaune de l'est.** Ste-Foy, QC: Ministère des Ressources naturelles du Québec, Direction des inventaires forestiers. 173 p.

53. Gosselin, J.; Grondin, P.; Saucier, J.-P. 1998. **Rapport de classification écologique du sous-domaine bioclimatique de la sapinière à bouleau jaune de l'ouest.** Ste-Foy, QC: Ministère des Ressources naturelles du Québec, Direction des inventaires forestiers. 163 p.

54. Gosselin, J.; Grondin, P.; Saucier, J.-P. 1999. **Rapport de classification écologique du sous-domaine bioclimatique de l'érablière à bouleau jaune de l'ouest.** Ste-Foy, QC: Ministère des Ressources naturelles du Québec, Direction des inventaires forestiers. 187 p.

55. Grondin, P.; Blouin, J.; Racine, P. 1999. **Rapport de classification écologique du sous-domaine bioclimatique de la sapinière à bouleau jaune de l'est.** Ste-Foy, QC: Ministère des Ressources naturelles du Québec, Direction des inventaires forestiers. 198 p.

56. Grondin, P.; Blouin, J.; Racine, P.; D'Avignon, H.; Tremblay, S. 1998. **Rapport de classification écologique du sous-domaine bioclimatique de la sapinière à bouleau blanc de l'est.** Ste-Foy, QC: Ministère des Ressources naturelles du Québec, Direction des inventaires forestiers. 261 p.

57. Heitzman, E.; Pregitzer, K.S.; Miller, R.O. 1997. **Origin and early development of northern white-cedar stands in northern Michigan.** Canadian Journal of Forest Research. 27: 1953-1961.

58. Heitzman, E.; Pregitzer, K.S.; Miller, R.O.; Lanasa, M.; Zuidema, M. 1999. **Establishment and development of northern white-cedar following strip clearcutting.** Forest Ecology and Management. 123: 97-104.

59. Hightshoe, G.L. 1978. **Native trees for urban and rural America - A planting design manual for environnemental designers.** Ames, IA: Iowa State University. 141 p.

60. Hofmeyer, P.V.; Seymour, R.S.; Kenefic, L.S. 2009. **Influence of soil site class on growth and decay of northern white-cedar and two associates in Maine.** Northern Journal of Applied Forestry. 26(2): 68-75.

61. Hofmeyer, P.V.; Seymour, R.S.; Kenefic, L.S. 2010. **Historical early stem development of northern white-cedar (***Thuja occidentalis*** L.) in Maine.** Northern Journal of Applied Forestry. 27(3): 92-96.

62. Hofmeyer, P.V.; Seymour, R.S.; Kenefic, L.S. 2010. **Production ecology of *Thuja occidentalis* L. in Maine.** Canadian Journal of Forest Research. 40: 1155-1164.

63. Holcombe, J.W. 1976. **The bryophyte flora of *Thuja* seedbed logs in a northern white-cedar swamp.** Michigan Botanist. 15: 173-181.

64. Holloway, G.L.; Naylor, B.J.; Watt, W.R. 2004. **Habitat relationships of wildlife in Ontario. Revised habitat suitability models for the Great Lakes-St. Lawrence and Boreal East forests.** Joint Tech. Rep. #1. Toronto, ON: Ontario Ministry of Natural Resources, Science and Information Branch, Southern Science and Information and Northeast Science and Information. 120 p.

65. Horton, J. 2011. **Personal communication.** NH Division of Forests & Lands. 172 Pembroke Rd., Concord, NH.

66. Hydro-Québec. 2005. **Répertoire des arbres et arbustes ornementaux.** 2e édition. Montréal, QC: Hydro-Québec Distribution. 547 p.

67. Jessome, A.P. 2000. **Résistance et propriétés connexes des bois indigènes au Canada.** Publ. SP-514F. Ste-Foy, QC: Forintek Canada Corp. 37 p.

68. Jobidon, R. 1995. **Autécologie de quelques espèces de compétition d'importance pour la régénération forestière au Québec - Revue de littérature.** Mémoire de recherche forestière no 117. Ste-Foy, QC: Gouvernement du Québec, Ministère des Ressources naturelles, Direction de la recherche forestière. 180 p.

69. Johnston, W.F. 1972. **Balsam fir dominant species under rethinned northern white-cedar.** Res. Note NC-133. St. Paul, MN: U.S. Department. of Agriculture, Forest Service, North Central Forest Experiment Station. 4 p.

70. Johnston, W.F. 1977. **Manager's handbook for white cedar in the north central states.** Gen. Tech. Rep. NC-35. St. Paul, MN: U.S. Department. of Agriculture, Forest Service, North Central Forest Experiment Station. 18 p.

71. Johnston, W.F. 1990. ***Thuja occidentalis* L. - northern white-cedar.** In: Burns, R.M.; Honkala, B.H., eds. Silvics of North America. Vol. 1. Agric. Hndbk. 654. Washington, DC: U.S. Department of Agriculture, Forest Service: 580-589.

72. Kell, J. 2009. **Soil-site influences on northern white-cedar (*Thuja occidentalis* L.) stem quality and growth.** Orono, ME: University of Maine. 75 p. M.S. thesis.

73. Lanasa, M.; Zuidema, M. 1991. **Site preparation for northern white-cedar.** Cedar note 2: Cedar evaluation development information and research. East Lansing, MI: Michigan State University. 6 p.

74. Larouche, C. 2006. **Raréfaction du thuya.** In: Grondin, P.; Cimon, A., eds. Les enjeux de biodiversité relatifs à la composition forestière. Chapitre 5 (Addenda). Ste-Foy, QC: Ministère des Ressources naturelles, de la Faune et des Parcs, Direction de la recherche forestière et Direction de l'environnement forestier. 32 p.

75. Larouche, C. 2007. **Examples of browsing impact on cedar.** Internal report. Québec, QC: Université Laval. 10 p. On file at Ministère des Ressources naturelles et de la Faune, Direction de la recherche forestière. 2700, rue Einstein, Québec, QC.

76. Larouche, C. 2009. **La régénération du thuya après coupes partielles en peuplements mixtes.** Québec, QC: Faculté de foresterie, géographie et géomatique, Université Laval. 158 p. Ph.D. thesis.

77. Larouche, C.; Kenefic, L.S.; Ruel, J.-C. 2010. **Northern white cedar regeneration dynamics on the Penobscot Experimental forest in Maine: 40 year results.** Northern Journal of Applied Forestry. 27(1): 5-12.

78. Larouche, C.; Morissette, S.; Ruel, J.-C.; Lussier, J.-M.; Kenefic, L.S. 2007. **Regeneration and growth of *Thuja occidentalis* in mixedwood stands after partial cutting.** In: Proceedings of the Carrefour de la recherche forestière. Carrefour de la recherche forestière; 2007 September 19-20; Québec, QC: 64-68. On file at Ministère des Ressources naturelles et de la Faune, Direction de la recherche forestière. 2700, rue Einstein. Québec, QC.

79. Larouche, C.; Ruel, J.-C.; Lussier, J.-M. 2011. **Factors affecting northern white-cedar (*Thuja occidentalis* L.) seedling establishment and early growth in mixedwood stands.** Canadian Journal of Forest Research. 41(3): 568-582.

80. Larson, D.W.; Kelly, P.E. 1991. **The extent of old-growth *Thuja occidentalis* on cliffs of the Niagara Escarpment.** Canadian Journal of Botany. 69: 1628-1636.

81. Larson, D.W.; Matthes-Sears, U.; Kelly, P.E. 1993. **Cambial dieback and partial shoot mortality in cliff-face *Thuja occidentalis*: Evidence for sectored radial architecture.** International Journal of Plant Sciences. 154: 496-505.

82. Lauriault, J. 1987. **Guide d'identification des arbres du Canada.** Montréal, QC: Musée national des sciences naturelles et Éditions Marcel Broquet. 551 p.

83. Leak, W.B.; Solomon, D.S.; DeBald, P.S. 1987. **Silviculture guide for northern hardwood types in the northeast. Revised edition.** Gen. Tech. Rep. NE-603. Upper Darby, PA: U.S. Department of Agriculture, Forest Service, Northeast Forest Experiment Station. 36 p.

84. LePage, P.T.; Canham, C.D.; Caoates, K.D.; Bartemucci, P. 2000. **Seed abundance versus substrate limitation of seeling recruitment in northern temperate forests of British Columbia.** Canadian Journal of Forest Research. 30: 415-427.

85. Lihra, T.; Ganev, S. 1999. **Machining properties of Eastern species and composite panels.** Project No. 2306. Québec, QC: Forintek Canada Corp. 62 p.

86. Lupien, P. 2004. **Des feuillus nobles en Basse-Mauricie. Guide de mise en valeur.** Shawinigan, QC: Syndicat des producteurs de bois de la Mauricie. 248 p.

87. Maine Forest Service. 2010. **2009 Wood processor report.** Augusta, ME: Department of Conservation, Maine Forest Service, Forest Policy and Management Division. 10 p. Available at www.maine.gov/doc/mfs/pubs/pdf/wdproc/09wdproc.pdf. (Accessed April 30, 2011).

88. McWilliams, W.H.; Butler, B.J.; Caldwell, L.E.; Griffith, D.M.; Hoppus, M.L.; Laustsen, K.M.; Lister, A.J.; Lister, T.W.; Metzler, J.W.; Morin, R.S.; Sader, S.A.; Stewart, L.B.; Steinman, J.R.; Westfall, J.A.; Williams, D.A.; Whitman, A.; Woodall, C.W. 2005. **The forests of Maine, 2003.** Resour. Bull. NE-164. Newtown Square, PA: U.S. Department of Agriculture, Forest Service, Northeastern Research Station. 188 p.

89. Meek, P.; Lussier, J.-M. 2006. **L'application du système des coupes progressives par une approche multitraitement pour l'aménagement des peuplements feuillus irréguliers de faible densité.** Montréal, QC: FERIC/Service canadien des forêts. 37 p.

90. Miller, B. 1995. **Autecology of black spruce.** Boreal mixedwood notes No. 9. Sault Ste.Marie, ON: Ontario Ministry of Natural Resources. 7 p.

91. Miller, R.O. 1990. **Ecology and management of northern white-cedar.** In: Regenerating conifer cover in deer yards: proceedings of a workshop; 1990 Dec. 4-5; North Bay, ON. North Bay, ON: Central Ontario Forest Technology Development Unit, Ministry of Natural Resources: 1-14.

92. Ministère des Ressources naturelles, de la Faune et des Parcs. 2003. **Manuel d'aménagement forestier, 4e édition.** Ste-Foy, QC: Direction des programmes forestiers du ministère des Ressources naturelles, de la Faune et des Parcs. 245 p.

93. Ministère des Ressources naturelles. 1995. **Petit manuel des semences forestières au Québec.** Ste-Foy, QC: Gouvernement du Québec, Ministère des Ressources naturelles. 72 p.

94. Ministère des Ressources naturelles. 1999. **Manuel de mise en valeur des forêts privées du Québec.** Ste-Foy, QC: Gouvernement du Québec, Ministère des Ressources naturelles. 180 p.

95. Musselman, R.C.; Lester, D.T.; Adams, M.S. 1975. **Localized ecotypes of *Thuja occidentalis* L. in Wisconsin.** Ecology. 56(3): 647-655.

96. Naser, B.; Bodinet, C.; Tegtmeier, M.; Lindequist, U. 2005. *Thuja occidentalis* **(Arbor vitae): A review of its pharmaceutical, pharmacological and clinical properties.** Evidence-Based Complementary and Alternative Medecine. 2(1): 69-78.

97. Natural Resources Conservation Service. 2011. **Plants database.** Greensboro, NC: U.S. Department of Agriculture, Natural Resources Conservation Service, National Plant Data Team. Available at http://plants.usda.gov/threat.html. (Accessed April 8, 2011).

98. NatureServe. 2011. **NatureServe explorer.** Arlington, VA: NatureServe. Available at http://www.natureserve.org/explorer/servlet/ NatureServe?init=Ecol. (Accessed April 8, 2011).

99. Nelson, T.C. 1951. **A reproduction study of northern white cedar including results of investigations under federal aid in wildlife restoration project Michigan 49-R.** Lansing, MI: Department of Conservation Game Divison. 100 p.

100. Nienstaedt, H.; Zasada, J.C. 1990. *Picea glauca* **(Moench) Voss. - white spruce.** In: Burns, R.M.; Honkala, B.H., eds. Silvics of North America. Vol. 1. Agric. Hndbk. 654. Washington, DC: U.S. Department of Agriculture, Forest Service: 204-226.

101. Nyland, R.D. 2002. **Silviculture: Concepts and applications.** New York, NY: McGraw-Hill Science/Engineering/Math. 633 p.

102. Ontario Ministry of Natural Resources. 1997. **Silvicultural guide to managing for black spruce, jack pine and aspen on boreal forest ecosites in Ontario.** Version 1.1. Toronto, ON: Ontario Ministry of Natural Resources. 822 p.

103. Ontario Ministry of Natural Resources. 1998. **A silvicultural guide for the Great Lakes- St. Lawrence conifer forest in Ontario.** Version 1.1. Toronto, ON: Ontario Ministry of Natural Resources. 424 p.

104. Ontario Ministry of Natural Resources. 2000. **A silvicultural guide to managing southern Ontario forests.** Toronto, ON: Ontario Ministry of Natural Resources. 654 p.

105. Ontario Ministry of Natural Resources. 2003. **Silviculture guide to managing spruce, fir, birch, and aspen mixedwoods in Ontario's boreal forest.** Toronto, ON: Ontario Ministry of Natural Resources. 382 p.

106. Ontario Ministry of Natural Resources. 2011. **Species at risk in Ontario (SARO) list.** Toronto, ON: Ontario Ministry of Natural Resources. Available at www.mnr.gov.on.ca/en/Business/Species/2ColumnSubPage/276722.html. (Accessed April 8, 2011).

107. Paquin, R.; Margolis, A.; Doucet, R.; Coyea, M.A. 1999. **Comparaison of growth and physiology of layers and naturally established seedlings of black spruce in a boreal cutover in Québec.** Canadian Journal of Forest Research. 29: 1-8.

108. Perala, D.A. 1990. *Populus tremuloides* **Michx. - quaking aspen.** In: Burns, R.M.; Honkala, B.H., eds. Silvics of North America. Vol. 2. Agric. Hndbk. 654. Washington, DC: U.S. Department of Agriculture, Forest Service: 555-569.

109. Perron, J.Y. 1985. **Tarif de cubage général - volume marchand brut.** Québec, QC: Gouvernement du Québec, Ministère de l'Énergie et des Ressources. 60 p.

110. Peterson, E.B.; Peterson, N.M. 1992. **Ecology, management and use of aspen and balsam poplar in the prairie provinces.** Spec. Rep. 1. Edmonton, AB: Forestry Canada, Northwest Region, Northern Forestry Centre. 252 p.

111. Pinto, F.; Romaniuk, S.; Ferguson, M. 2008. **Changes to pre-industrial forest tree composition in central and northeastern Ontario, Canada.** Canadian Journal of Forest Research. 38: 1842-1854.

112. Pothier, D.; Savard, F. 1998. **Actualisation des tables de production pour les principales espèces forestières du Québec.** Publ. no. RN98-3054. Québec, QC: Ministère des Ressources naturelles du Québec. 183 p.

113. Prévost, M. 1997. **Effects of scarification on seedbed coverage and natural regeneration after a group seed-tree cutting in a black spruce (*Picea mariana*) stand.** Forest Ecology and Management. 94: 219-231.

114. Raymond, P.; Bédard, S.; Roy, V.; Larouche, C.; Tremblay, S. 2009. **The irregular shelterwood system: review, classification, and potential application to forests affected by partial disturbances.** Journal of Forestry. 107(8): 405-413.

115. Rea, R.V. 2011. **Impacts of moose (*Alces alces*) browsing on paper birch (*Betula papyrifera*) morphology and potential timber quality.** Silva Fennica. 45(2): 227-236.

116. Roe, E.I. 1947. **Thinning in cedar swamp.** Tech. Note 279. St. Paul, MN: U.S. Department of Agriculture, Forest Service, Lake States Forest Experiment Station. 1 p.

117. Rooney, T.P.; Solheim, S.L.; Waller, D.M. 2002. **Factors affecting the regeneration of northern white cedar in lowland forests of the Upper Great Lakes region, USA.** Forest Ecology and Management. 163: 119-130.

118. Rose, A.H.; Lindquist, O.H. 1980. **Insectes du mélèze, du thuja et du génévrier de l'est du Canada.** Rap. Tech. 28F. Ottawa, ON: Ministère de l'Environnement, Service Canadien des Forêts. 100 p.

119. Sabine, D.L.; Morrison, S.F.; Whitlaw, H.A.; Ballard, W.B.; Forbes, G.J.; Bowman, J. 2002. **Migration behavior of white-tailed deer under varying winter climate regimes in New Brunswick.** Journal of Wildlife Management. 66(3): 718-728.

120. Safford, L.O.; Bjorkbom, J.C.; Zasada, J.C. 1990. *Betula papyrifera* **Marsh. - paper birch.** In: Burns, R.M.; Honkala, B.H., eds. Silvics of North America. Vol. 2. Agric. Hndbk. 654. Washington, DC: U.S. Department of Agriculture, Forest Service: 158-171.

121. Saucier, J.-P.; Gagné, C.; Bernier, S. 2007. **Indices de qualité de station des principales essences commerciales en fonction des types écologiques du Québec méridional.** Version: septembre 2007. Québec, QC: Ministère des Ressources naturelles et de la Faune, Direction des inventaires forestiers. 130 p.

122. Schaffer, W.W. 1996. **Silvicultural guidelines for the eastern white cedar.** Tech. Rep. TR-006. Peterborough, ON: Ontario Ministry of Natural Resources, Southern Region Science & Technology Transfer Unit. 62 p.

123. Schütz, J.-P. 1997. **Sylviculture 2 - La gestion des forêts irrégulières et mélangées.** Lausanne, Suisse: Presses Polytechniques et Universitaires Romandes. 168 p.

124. Scott, M.L.; Murphy, P.G. 1987. **Regeneration patterns of northern white cedar, an old-growth forest dominant.** American Midland Naturalist. 117: 10-16.

125. Seymour, R.S.; Guldin, J.; Marshall, D.; Palik, B. 2006. **Large-scale, long-term silvicultural experiments in the United States.** Allgemeine Forst Und Jagdseitung. 177(6/7): 104-112.

126. Seymour, R.S.; Hunter, M.L. 1999. **Principles of ecological forestry.** Chapter 2. In: Hunter, M.L., Jr., ed. Managing biodiversity in forest ecosystems. Cambridge, UK: Cambridge University Press: 22-61.

127. Seymour, R.S.; White, A.S.; deMaynadier, P.G. 2002. **Natural disturbance regimes in northeastern North America: Evaluating silvicultural systems using natural scales and frequencies.** Forest Ecology and Management. 155(2): 357-367.

128. Simard, M.-J.; Bergeron, Y.; Sirois, L. 2003. **Substrate and litterfall effects on conifer seedling survivorship in southern boreal stands of Canada.** Canadian Journal of Forest Research. 33: 672-681.

129. Sims, R.A.; Kershaw, H.M.; Wickware, G.M. 1990. **The autecology of major tree species in the North Central region of Ontario.** COFRDA Rep. 3302, NWOFTDU Tech. Rep. 48. Sault Ste. Marie, ON: Ontario Ministry of Natural Resources. 126 p.

130. Society of American Foresters. 2010. **Dictionary of forestry.** Bethesda, MD: Society of American Foresters. Available at http://dictionaryofforestry.org/. (Accessed December 2, 2010).

131. Ullrey, D.E.; Youatt, W.G.; Johnson, H.E.; Fay, L.D.; Brent, B.E. 1967. **Digestibility of cedar and jack pine browse for the white-tailed deer.** Journal of Wildlife Management. 31(3): 448-454.

132. Ullrey, D.E.; Youatt, W.G.; Johnson, H.E.;
     Fay, L.D.; Brent, B.E.; Kemp, K.E. 1968.
     **Digestibility of cedar and balsam fir browse
     for the white-tailed deer.** Journal of Wildlife
     Management. 32(1): 162-171.

133. Ullrey, D.E.; Youatt, W.G.; Johnson, H.E.; Ku,
     P.K.; Fay, L.D. 1964. **Digestibility of cedar and
     aspen browse for the white-tailed deer.** Journal
     of Wildlife Management. 28(4): 791-797.

134. Ung, C.-H.; Guo, X.J. 2011. **Canadian national
     taper equations.** Unpublished manuscript.
     St. Foy, Quebec, Canada: Natural Resources
     Canada, Canadian Forest Service, Laurentian
     Forestry Centre. 8 p.

135. Van Deelen, T.R. 1999. **Deer-cedar interaction
     during a period of mild winters: implications
     for conservation of conifer swamp deeryards
     in the Great Lakes region.** Natural Areas
     Journal. 19: 263-274.

136. Verme, L.J.; Johnston, W.F. 1986. **Regeneration
     of northern white cedar deeryards in upper
     Michigan.** Journal of Wildlife Management.
     50: 307-313.

137. Waiters, R.S.; Yawney, H.M. 1990. *Acer rubrum
     L. - red maple.* In: Burns, R.M.; Honkala, B.H.,
     eds. Silvics of North America. Vol. 2. Agric.
     Hndbk. 654. Washington, DC: U.S. Department
     of Agriculture, Forest Service: 60-69.

138. Watkins, L. 2011. **The forest resource of
     Ontario 2011.** Sault Ste. Marie, ON: Ontario
     Ministry of Natural Resources. 307 p.

139. Wein, R.W.; Moore, J.M. 1979. **Fire history
     and recent fire rotation periods in the Nova
     Scotia Acadian forest.** Canadian Journal of
     Forest Research. 9(2): 285-294.

140. Weiskittel, A.R.; Hofmeyer, P.V.; Seymour, R.S.
     2010. **Modelling primary branch frequency
     and size for five conifer species in Maine,
     USA.** Forest Ecology and Management. 259:
     1912-1921.

141. Weiskittel, A.R.; Kenefic, L.S.; Seymour,
     R.S.; Phillips, L.M. 2009. **Long-term effects
     of precommercial thinning on the stem
     dimensions, form and branch characteristics
     of red spruce and balsam fir crop trees in
     Maine, USA.** Silva Fennica. 43(3):397-409.

142. Wilson, G.F.; Maguire, D.A. 1996. **Simulation
     of early regeneration processes in mixed-
     species forests of Maine, USA: germination,
     survival, and height growth.** In: Skorsgaard,
     J.P.; Johannsen, V.K., eds. Modeling regression
     success and early growth of forest stands.
     Horsholm, Denmark: Danish Forest and
     Landscape Research Institute: 530-539.

143. Zhang, Q.; Pregitzer, K.S.; Reed, D.D. 1999.
     **Catastrophic disturbance in the presettlement
     forests of the Upper Peninsula of Michigan.**
     Canadian Journal of Forest Research. 29:
     106-114.

Tree Size and Growth

Reference Values for Diameter Increment

Reference values of diameter increment provide data on superior, average and inferior increment in relation to tree diameter (Fig. 11). These values are based on permanent plot data from eastern Canada and the northeastern United States.[4,5]

---

[4] Permanent plot data from the United Sates are from the U.S. Forest Service FIA database for Maine, Vermont, New Hampshire, and New York. Permanent plot data from the Provinces of Quebec, New Brunswick, Nova Scotia, and Prince Edward Island were also used.

[5] The average growth level corresponds to an increment between the 33rd and 67th percentiles of d.b.h. increment. The inferior growth level corresponds to increment value lower than the 33rd percentile, while for the superior growth level, increment is higher than the 67th percentile.

Increment reference values can be used to:

1. Assess tree or stand growth:

By coring trees and measuring the number of tree rings over the last centimeter (0.5 in) of growth, one can determine if a tree has average, superior, or inferior diameter growth relative to other trees in its diameter class.

At the stand scale, the average values of d.b.h. and increment can be calculated to assess overall stand growth.

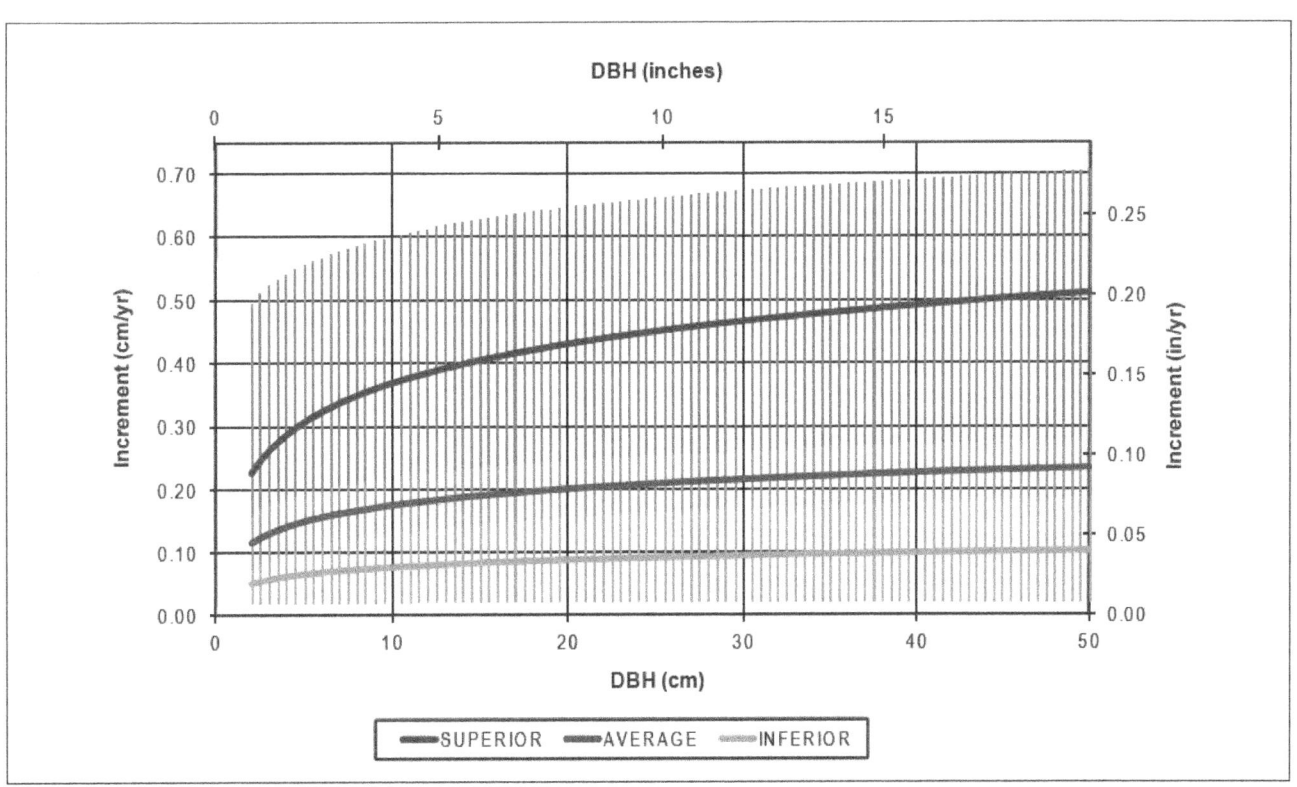

Figure 11.—Reference values of diameter increment of cedar. Figure by Jean-Martin Lussier and Aaron Weiskittel, used with permission.

In the field, diameter increment can quickly be measured using the time of passage[6] (Table 7). The current time of passage of a tree is estimated by the number of the tree rings over the last centimeter (0.5 in) of growth near the bark (considering 2-cm or 1-inch d.b.h. classes).

A simple way to compare trees with different diameter is to use a **relative growth index**, which is computed by dividing the measured increment by the average reference value of increment for that diameter class. For example, a 20-cm tree with a d.b.h. increment of

0.3 cm/yr has a growth index of 0.3/0.2 = 1.5, since the average increment of a tree of similar size is 0.2 cm/yr (Fig. 11). This means that this tree is growing 1.5 times faster than the average. An assessment can be done at the stand level by using the average d.b.h. increment and the average d.b.h. of the stand.

Diameter growth is influenced by genetic, climatic, site, and biologic factors (such as competition, predation, or disease), and it is difficult to relate tree or stand growth to a single factor. However, reference values can be useful for monitoring tree and stand growth and for expressing growth in a meaningful way for silviculture decisions.

---

[6] Mathematically, the time of passage is equal to w/i_d, where w is the range of the diameter class and i_d the annual increment in the same units.

Table 7.—Time of passage for cedar with superior, average, and inferior diameter growth

METRIC				ENGLISH			
	Years for 2-cm increase in diameter				Years for 1-in increase in diameter		
d.b.h. (cm)	Superior	Average	Inferior	d.b.h. (in)	Superior	Average	Inferior
2	<13	13-27	>27	1	<15	15-31	>31
4	<11	11-20	>20	2	<13	13-24	>24
6	<10	10-18	>18	3	<12	12-21	>21
8	<9	9-16	>16	4	<12	12-19	>19
10	<9	9-15	>15	5	<11	11-18	>18
12	<9	9-15	>15	6	<11	11-18	>18
14	<9	9-14	>14	7	<11	11-17	>17
16	<8	8-14	>14	8	<10	10-16	>16
18	<8	8-13	>13	9	<10	10-16	>16
20	<8	8-13	>13	10	<10	10-16	>16
22	<8	8-13	>13	11	<10	10-15	>15
24	<8	8-12	>12	12	<10	10-15	>15
26	<8	8-12	>12	13	<10	10-15	>15
28	<8	8-12	>12	14	<10	10-15	>15
30	<8	8-12	>12	15	<9	9-14	>14
32	<8	8-12	>12	16	<9	9-14	>14
34	<8	8-12	>12	17	<9	9-14	>14
36	<8	8-11	>11	18	<9	9-14	>14
38	<7	7-11	>11	19	<9	9-14	>14
40	<7	7-11	>11	20	<9	9-14	>14
42	<7	7-11	>11	21	<9	9-13	>13
44	<7	7-11	>11	22	<9	9-13	>13
46	<7	7-11	>11	23	<9	9-13	>13
48	<7	7-11	>11	24	<9	9-13	>13
50	<7	7-11	>11	25	<9	9-13	>13

2. Make assumptions about future growth

Because tree mortality is related to vigor, it is possible to make reasonable assumptions about the expected survival rate of trees knowing their size and current increment.

If we assume that a tree or stand will maintain the same relative growth[7] (i.e., the same average reference value), we can use Figure 11 to estimate future growth of trees and the time required to produce a desirable tree size (Fig. 12).

[7] This assumption is reasonable if we consider broad classes of growth rates; at this time, no better model is available.

Here is an example of this application: A forest manager wants to estimate the length of time needed to produce high value cedar trees of 30 cm d.b.h. A 9-cm (4-in) tree will need 50, 110, or 250 years to reach this target d.b.h. depending on its growth (Fig. 12). Moreover, to take expected mortality into account, the forester will need to ensure recruitment of 1.1 trees from the sapling to pole stage in order to produce a single 30-cm (12-in) tree at the average growth rate. If the growth level is low, six trees need to be recruited to assure the same target. In the case of trees with superior growth, this ratio is about 1 to 1 due to negligible mortality.

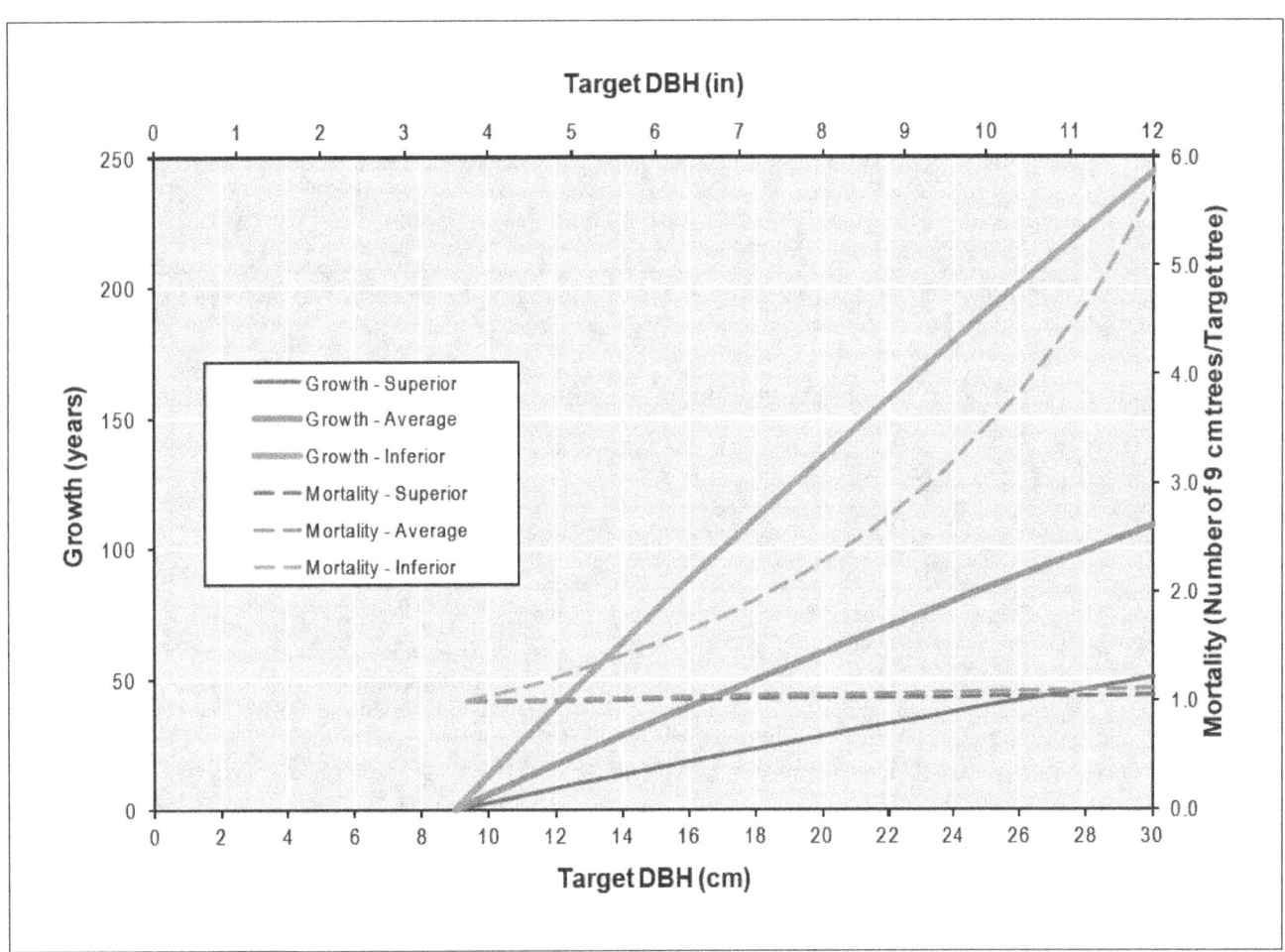

Figure 12.—Average time required to reach a target d.b.h. and mortality of a 9-cm cedar tree, for three levels of increment. (Mortality rates are expressed as the number of 9-cm [or 4-in] trees needed for producing a target tree of a given diameter.) Figure by Jean-Martin Lussier and Aaron Weiskittel, used with permission.

Stem Form, Volume, and Log Yield

A model demonstrating the relation between tree d.b.h. and height for cedar was developed recently (134) (Fig. 13). Based on permanent plot data from eastern Canada and the northeastern United States, tree-level merchantable volume equations (Table 8) and the relation between tree d.b.h. and maximum log length for cedar were computed (Fig. 14).

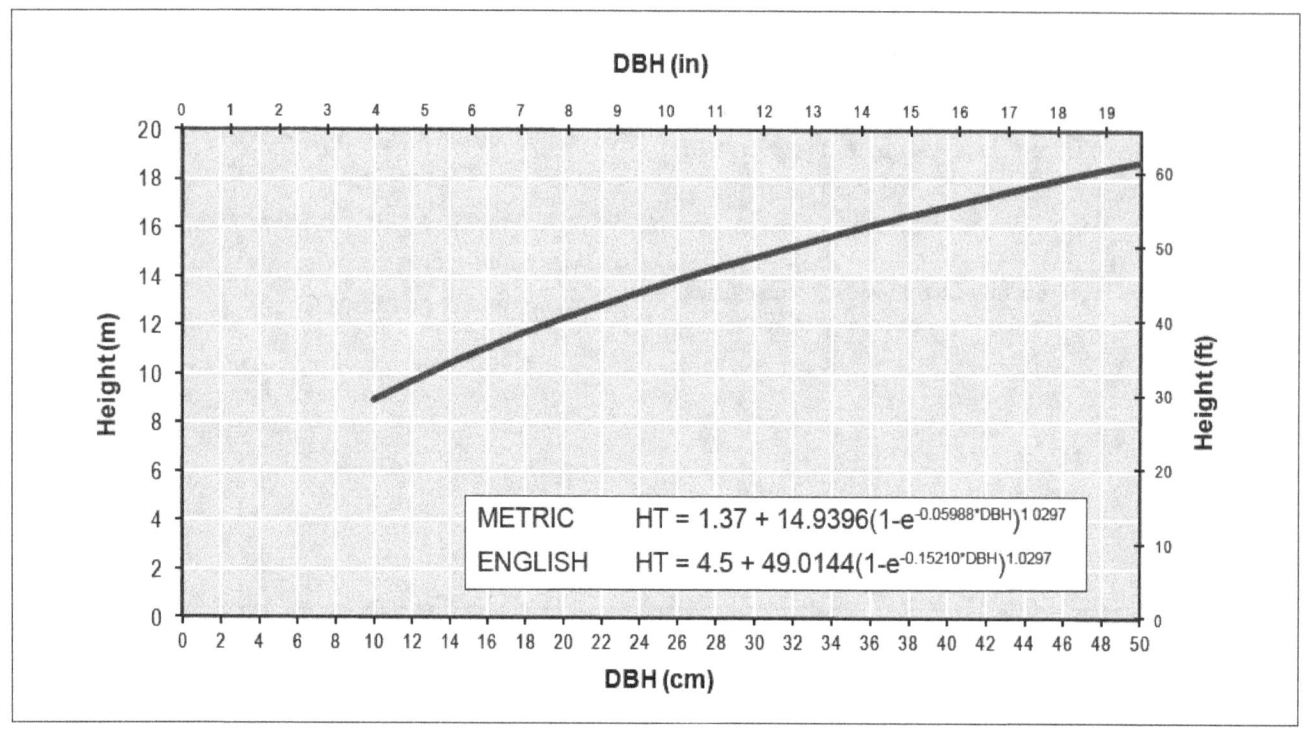

| METRIC | HT = 1.37 + 14.9396(1-e$^{-0.05988*DBH}$)$^{1.0297}$ |
| ENGLISH | HT = 4.5 + 49.0144(1-e$^{-0.15210*DBH}$)$^{1.0297}$ |

Figure 13.—Relation between cedar tree d.b.h and height (134). Figure by Jean-Martin Lussier and Aaron Weiskittel, used with permission.

Table 8.—Tree and stand-level merchantable volume equations for cedar (for a minimum d.b.h. of 9 cm or 4 in)

Scale	Unit system	Equation	Variables	Reference
Tree	Metric	$V = 0.03224\ D^2 - 4.14505\ H + 0.39731\ DH + 0.01995\ D^2H$	V = merchantable volume (dm³) H = total height (m) D = d.b.h. (cm)	109
	English	$V = 0.00735\ D^2 - 0.04462\ H + 0.01086\ DH + 0.00139\ D^2H$	V = merchantable volume (ft³) H = total height (ft) D = d.b.h. (in)	
Stand	Metric	$V = 0.53095 \times H^{0.42474} \times G^{0.9044} \times D_q^{0.47797}$	V = merchantable volume (m³/ha) H = dominant height (m) D_q = quadratic mean d.b.h. (cm) G = basal area (m²/ha)	112
	English	$V = 1.8901 \times H^{0.42474} \times G^{0.9044} \times D_q^{0.47797}$	V = merchantable volume (ft³/ac) H = dominant height (ft) D_q = quadratic mean d.b.h. (in) G = basal area (ft²/ac)	

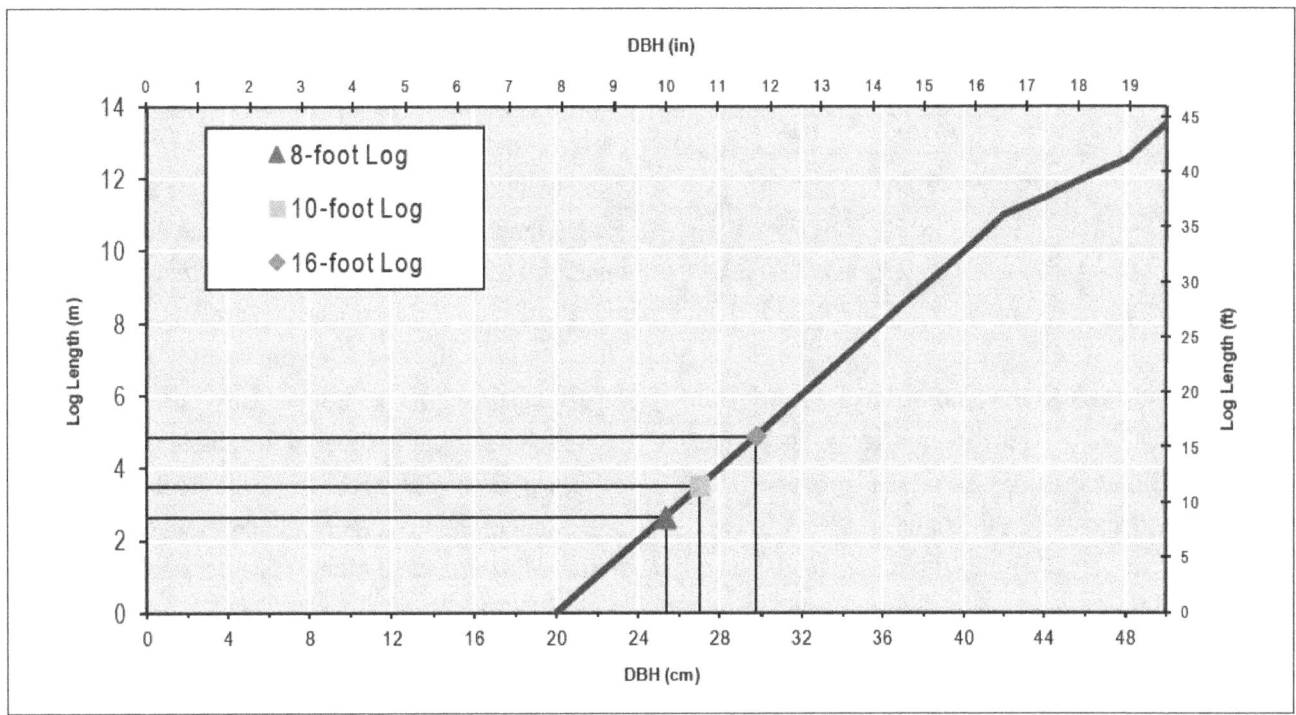

Figure 14.—Relation between cedar tree d.b.h. and maximum log length (log minimum diameter of 22 cm [8.5 in]). Figure by Jean-Martin Lussier and Aaron Weiskittel, used with permission.

Stand Dynamics

Stand structure changes over time due to tree growth and demographic changes (regeneration and mortality). Most silviculture actions try to modify stand dynamics to achieve management goals.

Size-class models represent the stand in terms of the distribution of trees among size-classes. For practical purposes, we propose the **size class definitions** on Table 9. A "large tree" corresponds to an individual that will likely have one 16-foot log with a small-end diameter 22 cm (9 in) or larger. According to

forest inventory data, 90 percent of cedar trees in the northeastern United States and adjacent Canada have a d.b.h. less than or equal to 29 cm (11 in).

Annual tree mortality has been compiled from permanent plot data from the eastern United States and the province of Quebec, for each size class (Table 10). Cedar mortality is correlated with tree growth. In general, mortality is low (<0.2 percent) for trees with average and superior growth. Trees with inferior growth have higher mortality rates, which increase with tree size. No data were available for saplings (i.e., d.b.h. $\leq$ 9 cm [3.5 in]).

Table 9.—Definitions of size classes

Tree size class	Metric (cm)			English (in)		
	Minimum d.b.h.	Maximum d.b.h.	D.b.h. Classes	Minimum d.b.h.	Maximum d.b.h.	D.b.h Classes
Small	9	19	10,12,14,16,18	3.5	8.5	4-5-6-7
Medium	19	29	20-22-24-26-28	8.5	12.5	8-9-10-11
Large	29		30+	12.5		12+

Table 10.—Average mortality rates for cedar by tree size class and d.b.h. increment level

Tree Size Class	D.b.h. Increment Level		
	Inferior	Average	Superior
Small	0.68%	0.08%	0.11%
Medium	0.73%	0.14%	0.08%
Large	1.16%	0.11%	0.14%

Mortality statistics can be combined with growth data (Fig. 13) to calculate **transition matrices**. For a given time period, these matrices provide the probability that a tree will stay within the same size class, grow into a larger size class, or die. Table 11 gives 10-year transition probabilities for stands of inferior, average, and superior growth. The interpretation of these matrices is quite straightforward. For example, in average conditions, a small tree (9 cm [3.5 in] $\leq$ d.b.h. < 19 cm [8.5 in]) over 10 years has 80.8 percent chance of remaining in the same size class and 18.5 percent chance of growing to the medium size class.

Table 11.—Ten-year transition matrices for cedar for three growth classes

Inferior Growth		Initial Stage		
		Small	Medium	Large
Stage at the end of the period	Small	0.869	<0.001	<0.001
	Medium	0.079	0.844	<0.001
	Large	0.000	0.085	0.890

Average Growth		Initial Stage		
		Small	Medium	Large
Stage at the end of the period	Small	0.808	<0.001	<0.001
	Medium	0.185	0.782	<0.001
	Large	0.000	0.204	0.989

Superior Growth		Initial Stage		
		Small	Medium	Large
Stage at the end of the period	Small	0.597	<0.001	<0.001
	Medium	0.396	0.547	<0.001
	Large	0.000	0.445	0.986

The sum of the two probabilities is equal to 99.3 percent: this means that the probability of dying is 0.7 percent (100 minus 99.3 percent).

The evolution of stands over time can be easily modeled on a spreadsheet as long as the user has an inventory of the number of trees per size class per area unit (18).

Ingrowth is the last (but not the least) component of a size-class model. It is equal to the number of saplings that are periodically reaching the minimal commercial size (9 cm or 3.5 in). Figure 15 shows ingrowth data from 7,566 permanent plots in eastern Canada and United States.

Results show that no ingrowth was recorded on 87 percent of the sample plots (Fig. 15). Only 1 percent of the plots had an ingrowth rate over 150 stems/ha/yr (61 stems/ac/yr) and 95 percent of the plots had an ingrowth rate equal to or lower than 12 trees/ha/yr (5 trees/ac/yr).

Ingrowth is a highly variable process and most models do not provide precise predictions. Using regeneration inventory data, it is possible to make rough estimates,

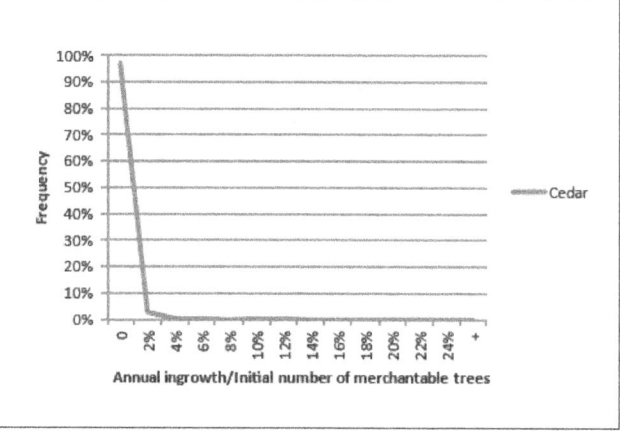

Figure 15.—Frequency of the annual ingrowth for cedar based on permanent plot data from eastern Canada and the northeastern United States. Figure by Jean-Martin Lussier and Aaron Weiskittel, used with permission.

considering the time required for sapling classes to reach a merchantable size (Table 12). For example, if we have 50 saplings/ha of 6 cm (2.4 in) d.b.h., we can expect ingrowth within the next 10 years of between 14 and 27 trees/ha (respectively, 50 × 29% and 50 × 53%). These estimations are of course quite optimistic because they do not take in account sapling mortality, which is unknown.

Yield Tables for Even-age Management

Site index curves (Fig. 16) and yield tables (Table 13) for cedar in Quebec were developed (112).

Table 12.—Time needed for sapling promotion to the pole-timber class and the corresponding gross promotion rates for a 10-year period (without mortality)

Sapling d.b.h. class	Years to pole class	Gross 10-year promotion rate of saplings to pole class	Sapling d.b.h. class	Years to pole class	Gross 10-year promotion rate of saplings to pole class
— Metric —			— English —		
2 cm	42-81 yrs	12-24%	1 in	40-76 yrs	13-25%
4 cm	29-54 yrs	19-34%	2 in	25-45 yrs	22-40%
6 cm	19-34 yrs	29-53%	3 in	12-21 yrs	48-83%
8 cm	9-16 yrs	63-100%			

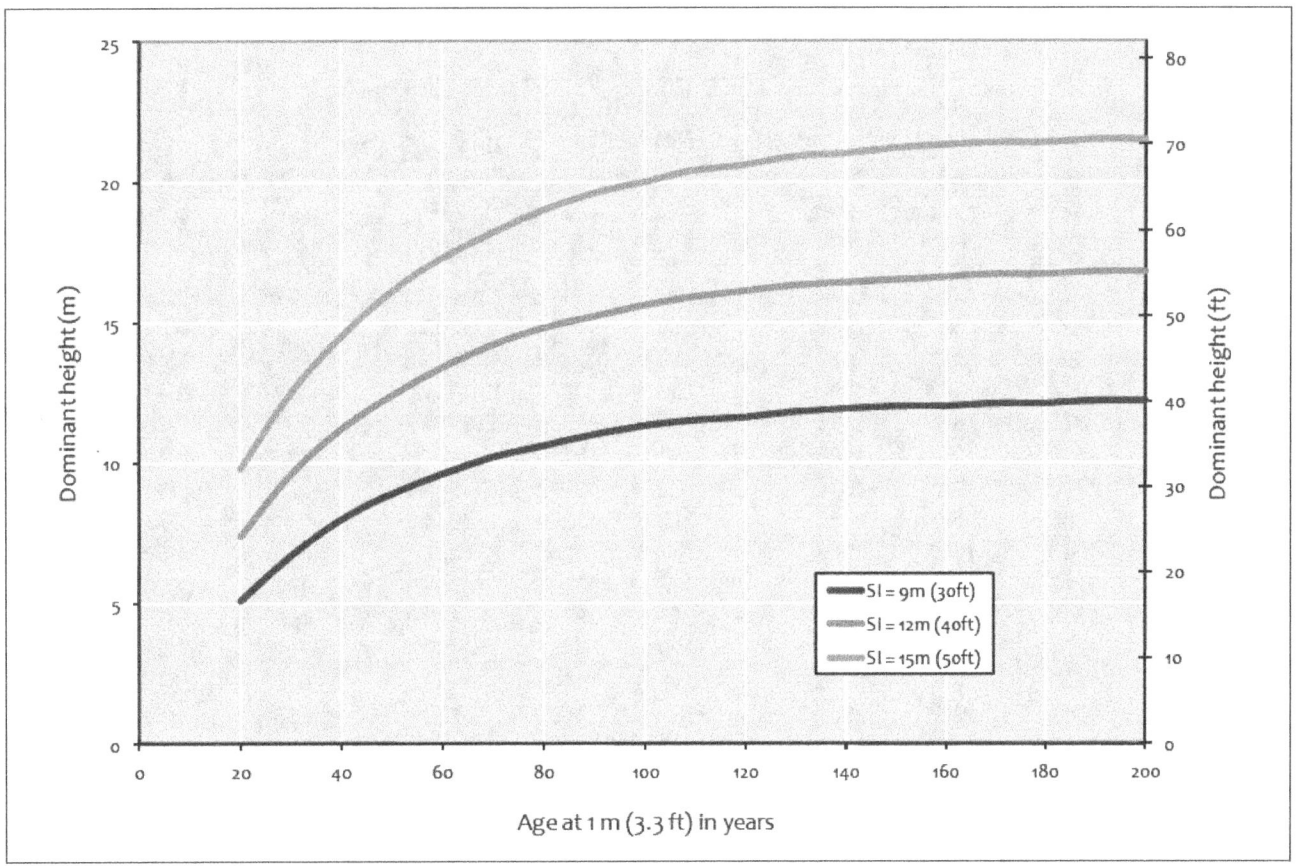

Figure 16.—Site index curves for cedar (112). Figure by Jean-Martin Lussier and Aaron Weiskittel, used with permission.

Table 13.—Yield tables for cedar [a,b] (merchantable volume for a diameter over 9 cm) (112)

METRIC

Gross Merchantable Volume (over 9 cm [3.5 in] in diameter, in m³/ha)

Stand age at ht = 1m (yr)	Site Index (50 yrs) = 9 m			Site Index (50 yrs) = 12 m			Site Index (50 yrs) = 15 m		
	Low Density	Average Density	High Density	Low Density	Average Density	High Density	Low Density	Average Density	High Density
20	0	2	8	2	11	33	23	43	72
30	2	9	25	12	36	77	66	100	140
40	7	23	47	30	69	121	114	157	201
50	15	39	70	53	102	161	160	206	252
60	26	57	92	77	134	195	200	247	292
70	37	74	111	101	162	224	235	282	325
80	50	90	129	124	187	248	265	310	351
90	62	105	144	145	209	269	290	334	373
100	73	118	158	164	228	286	312	354	392
110	85	130	170	181	245	301	331	371	407
120	95	141	180	197	260	313	347	386	420
130	105	151	189	211	272	324	362	399	431
140	114	160	197	223	283	333	373	409	439
150	122	167	203	230	287	333	376	410	438
160	127	171	205	229	282	324	368	399	425
170	128	169	200	220	268	306	349	376	399
180	124	162	190	203	245	277	318	341	360
190	115	148	172	177	210	237	272	291	307
200	101	128	148	139	164	183	211	225	237

ENGLISH

Gross Merchantable Volume (over 9 cm [3.5 in] in diameter, in ft³/ac)

Stand age at ht = 3.3 ft (yr)	Site Index (50 yrs) = 30 ft			Site Index (50 yrs) = 40 ft			Site Index (50 yrs) = 50 ft		
	Low Density	Average Density	High Density	Low Density	Average Density	High Density	Low Density	Average Density	High Density
20	0	29	114	29	157	472	329	615	1029
30	29	129	357	171	514	1100	943	1429	2001
40	100	329	672	429	986	1729	1629	2244	2873
50	214	557	1000	757	1458	2301	2287	2944	3601
60	372	815	1315	1100	1915	2787	2858	3530	4173
70	529	1058	1586	1443	2315	3201	3358	4030	4645
80	715	1286	1844	1772	2672	3544	3787	4430	5016
90	886	1501	2058	2072	2987	3844	4144	4773	5331
100	1043	1686	2258	2344	3258	4087	4459	5059	5602
110	1215	1858	2430	2587	3501	4302	4730	5302	5817
120	1358	2015	2572	2815	3716	4473	4959	5516	6002
130	1501	2158	2701	3015	3887	4630	5173	5702	6160
140	1629	2287	2815	3187	4044	4759	5331	5845	6274
150	1744	2387	2901	3287	4102	4759	5374	5859	6260
160	1815	2444	2930	3273	4030	4630	5259	5702	6074
170	1829	2415	2858	3144	3830	4373	4988	5374	5702
180	1772	2315	2715	2901	3501	3959	4545	4873	5145
190	1644	2115	2458	2530	3001	3387	3887	4159	4387
200	1443	1829	2115	1986	2344	2615	3015	3216	3387

[a] These yield tables assume the stand will collapse at around 160-180 years (shaded areas). However, this hypothesis is questionable because no long-term data support it.

[b] The original reference also provides estimates for saw log volume (for diameter over 13 cm [5 in] and 17 cm [7 in]).

S1 : UPLAND
STANDS ON VERY THIN SOIL OR OUTCROPS

SITE DESCRIPTION

Ecological Classification

Refer to Appendix III

Physical Environment

Topographic location:
Upper slope, hill top, and escarpment

Soil depth and moisture
Very thin soil (< 25 cm [10 in]), often with rock outcrops

Texture	Humidity			
	Dry (excessively drained)	Fresh (well drained)	Moist (imperfectly drained)	Very moist - wet (poorly drained)
Very shallow, outcrop	•	•	•	n.a.
Coarse (sand)				
Loamy (glacial till)				
Clayed				
Organic	n.a.	n.a.	n.a.	

Vegetation Description

● Tolerant hardwood, mixed-wood, and softwood stands where cedar is a minor component

● Softwood stands where cedar is a significant companion species (fir stands with cedar) or is a minor component

Example of main companion species:

Hardwood: yellow and white birch, sugar and red maple, poplar

Softwood: balsam fir, red, white and black spruce, eastern hemlock, white and jack pine

Left: Spruce and fir stand on very thin soil. Photo by Guy Lessard, CERFO, used with permission.

Right: Yellow birch and fir stand on very thin soil. Photo by Guy Lessard, CERFO, used with permission.

MAIN CONSTRAINTS

Suitable Management Objectives

- **Low** (softwood stands) **to moderate** (mixed-wood and hardwood stands) timber production potential

- **Biodiversity**

Level of Competition

Mixed-wood and hardwood stands:

Softwood stands:

Trafficability Constraints

Slope 15-30%:

Slope 30-40%:   !

Terrain roughness: !

Soil Fragility

Slope 15-40%:   !

In all conditions: !

Risk of Windthrow

In all conditions: !

Caution

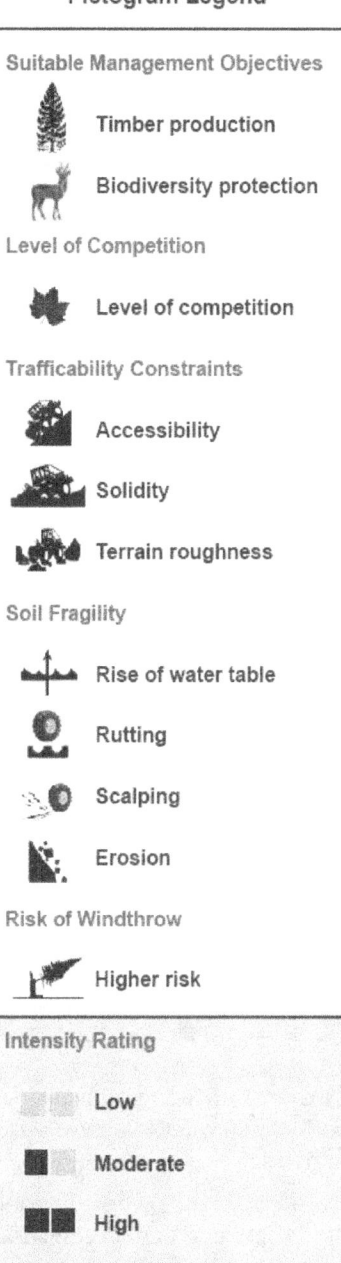

Pictogram Legend

Suitable Management Objectives

- Timber production
- Biodiversity protection

Level of Competition

- Level of competition

Trafficability Constraints

- Accessibility
- Solidity
- Terrain roughness

Soil Fragility

- Rise of water table
- Rutting
- Scalping
- Erosion

Risk of Windthrow

- Higher risk

Intensity Rating

- Low
- Moderate
- High
- Very high

S2: UPLAND
STANDS ON DRY OR FRESH DEEP SOILS

SITE DESCRIPTION

Ecological Classification

Refer to Appendix III

Physical Environment

Topographic location:
Upper to mid-slope

Soil depth and moisture
Frequently thin (25-50 cm [10-20 in]) to deep (> 50 cm [20 in]) soil

Texture	Humidity			
	Dry (excessively drained)	Fresh (well drained)	Moist (imperfectly drained)	Very moist - wet (poorly drained)
Very shallow, outcrop				n.a.
Coarse (sand)	•	•		
Loamy (glacial till)	•	•		
Clayed	•	•		
Organic	n.a.	n.a.	n.a.	

Vegetation Description

● Tolerant hardwood and mixed-wood stands where cedar is a minor component

● Softwood stands where cedar is a significant companion species (fir stands with cedar) or is a minor component

Example of main companion species:

Hardwood: yellow and white birch, sugar and red maple, poplar

Softwood: balsam fir, red, white and black spruce, eastern hemlock, white pine

Top: Yellow birch and fir stand on deep fresh soil. Photo by Guy Lessard, CERFO, used with permission. Right: Cedar and fir stand on deep fresh soil. Photo by Jocelyn Gosselin, MRNF, used with permission.

MAIN CONSTRAINTS

Suitable Management Objectives

- **Moderate** (softwood stands) **to high** (mixed-wood and hardwood stands) timber production potential

- **Biodiversity**

Caution

Level of Competition

Mixed-wood and hardwood stands:    !

Softwood stands:

Trafficability Constraints

Slope 15-30%: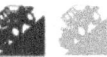

Slope 30-40%:      !

Terrain roughness:

Soil Fragility

Seepage:

Slope 15-60% and thin soil:

Slope 30-40% and thin soil:    !

Thin soil (25-50 cm [10-20 in]):

Clayed soil:

Risk of Windthrow

Thin soil (25-50 cm [10-20 in]):      !

Deep soil (>50 cm [20 in])

Pictogram Legend

Suitable Management Objectives

 Timber production

 Biodiversity protection

Level of Competition

 Level of competition

Trafficability Constraints

 Accessibility

 Solidity

 Terrain roughness

Soil Fragility

 Rise of water table

 Rutting

 Scalping

 Erosion

Risk of Windthrow

 Higher risk

Intensity Rating

 Low

Moderate

High

 Very high

S3: LOWLAND
STANDS ON MOIST DEEP MINERAL SOILS

SITE DESCRIPTION

Ecological Classification

Refer to Appendix III

Physical Environment

Topographic location:
Lower slope, depression and flat ground

Soil depth and moisture
Thin (25-50 cm [10-20 in]) to deep (> 50 cm [20 in]) soil

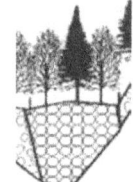

Texture	Humidity			
	Dry (excessively drained)	Fresh (well drained)	Moist (imperfectly drained)	Very moist - wet (poorly drained)
Very shallow, outcrop				n.a.
Coarse (sand)			●	
Loamy (glacial till)			●	
Clayed			●	
Organic	n.a.	n.a.	n.a.	

Vegetation Description

● Tolerant hardwood and mixed-wood stands where cedar is a minor component

● Softwood stands where cedar is a significant companion species (fir stands with cedar) or is a minor component

Example of main companion species:

Hardwood: yellow and white birch, sugar and red maple, poplar

Softwood: balsam fir, red, white and black spruce, eastern hemlock, white pine

Left: Yellow birch and fir stand on deep moist soil. Right: Cedar and fir stand on deep moist soil. Photos by Jocelyn Gosselin, MRNF, used with permission.

MAIN CONSTRAINTS

Suitable Management Objectives

- **Moderate** (softwood stands) **to high** (mixed-wood and hardwood stands) timber production potential

- **Biodiversity**

Pictogram Legend

Suitable Management Objectives

 Timber production

 Biodiversity protection

Level of Competition

 Level of competition

Trafficability Constraints

 Accessibility

 Solidity

 Terrain roughness

Soil Fragility

 Rise of water table

 Rutting

 Scalping

 Erosion

Risk of Windthrow

 Higher risk

Intensity Rating

 Low

 Moderate

 High

Very high

Caution

Level of Competition

Mixed-wood and hardwood stands:  !

Softwood stands:

Trafficability Constraints

Slope 15-30%:

Terrain roughness:

Soil Fragility

Seepage:

Slope 15-30% and thin soil:

Thin soil (25-50 cm [10-20 in]):

Clayed soil: !

Coarse or loamy soil:

In all conditions:  !

Risk of Windthrow

Thin soil (25-50 cm [10-20 in]):  !

Deep soil (>50 cm [20 in]):

S4: LOWLAND
STANDS ON VERY MOIST DEEP MINERAL OR ORGANIC SOILS

SITE DESCRIPTION

Ecological Classification

Refer to Appendix III

Physical Environment

Topographic location:
Upper slope, depression and flat ground

Soil depth and moisture
Frequently deep deposits (> 50 cm [20 in])

	Humidity			
Texture	Dry (excessively drained)	Fresh (well drained)	Moist (imperfectly drained)	Very moist - wet (poorly drained)
Very shallow, outcrop				n.a.
Coarse (sand)				•
Loamy (glacial till)				•
Clayed				•
Organic	n.a.	n.a.	n.a.	•

Vegetation Description

- Tolerant hardwood and mixed-wood stands where cedar is a minor component

- Softwood stands where cedar is a significant companion species (fir stands with cedar, cedar stands) or is a minor component

Example of main companion species:

Hardwood: white and yellow birch, black ash, red maple

Softwood: balsam fir, red and black spruce

Top: Cedar stand on deep mineral very moist soil. Right: Spruce stand on deep organic very moist soil. Photos by Jocelyn Gosselin, MRNF, used with permission.

MAIN CONSTRAINTS

Suitable Management Objectives

√ **Low** (softwood stands without underground water circulation) **to moderate** (softwood, hardwood and mixed-wood stands with underground water circulation) timber production potential

√ **Biodiversity**

Level of Competition

Mixed-wood and hardwood stands:

Softwood stands:

Trafficability Constraints

In all conditions:

Soil Fragility

Clayed or organic soil:

Coarse or loamy soil:

In all conditions:

Risk of Windthrow

In all conditions:

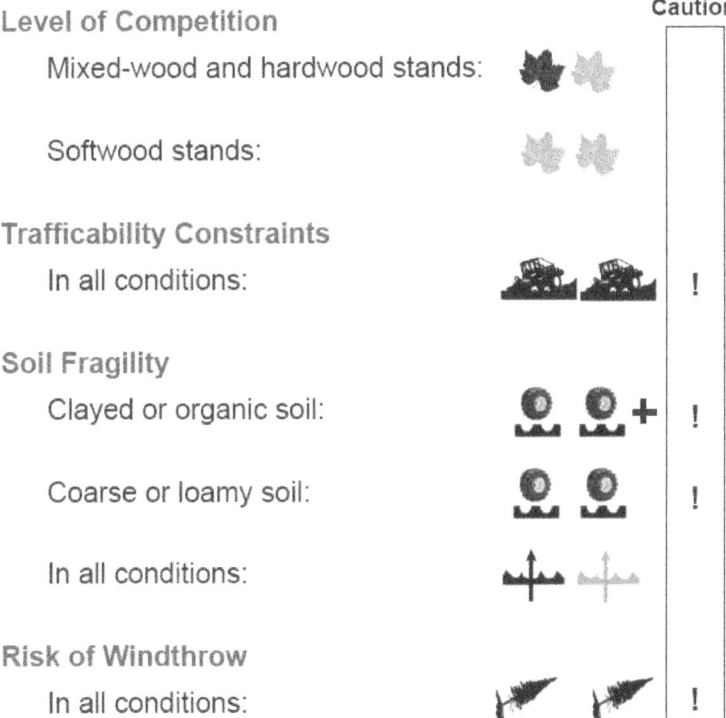

Caution

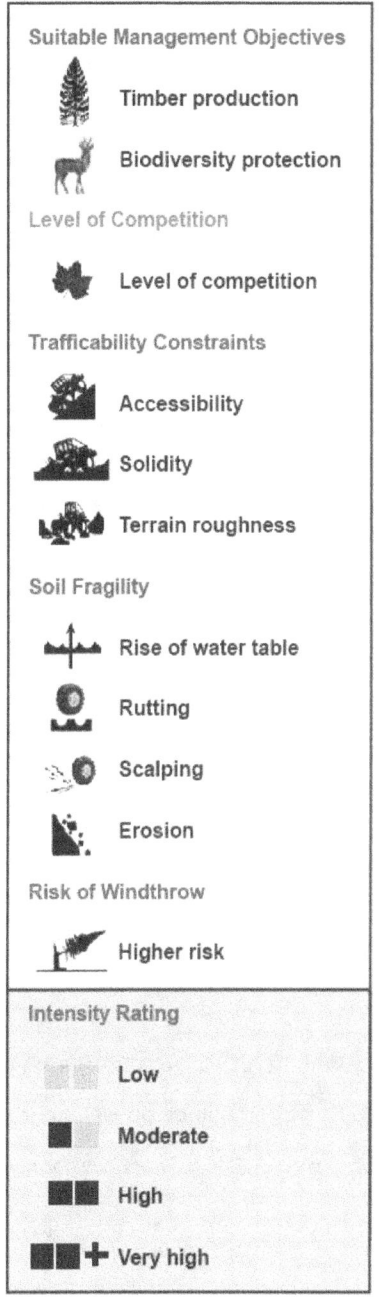

Pictogram Legend

Suitable Management Objectives

Timber production

Biodiversity protection

Level of Competition

Level of competition

Trafficability Constraints

Accessibility

Solidity

Terrain roughness

Soil Fragility

Rise of water table

Rutting

Scalping

Erosion

Risk of Windthrow

Higher risk

Intensity Rating

Low

Moderate

High

Very high

S1 UPLAND: Stands on Very Thin Soil or Outcrops

	North American Associations (98)[a]	Quebec Classification (Ecological types) (52-56)	Ontario Classification (Ecosites) (3)
S1.1. Upland stands on very thin soils (very well drained soils)			
Typical sites	2451: *Thuja occidentalis*; cliff woodland 5126: *Pinus banksiana, Thuja occidentalis, Picea glaucal Juniperus communis*; woodland 6021: *Thuja occidentalisl Carex eburnean*; forest	MS20: Fir, white birch; very thin soils MS60: Fir, red maple; very thin soils RE20: Black spruce with feathermoss or ericaceous shrubs; very thin soils RP10: White or red pine; very thin soils RS10: Fir, cedar; very thin soils RS20: Fir, black spruce; very thin soils RS50: Fir, red spruce; very thin soils	G013: Hemlock-cedar conifer; very shallow, dry to fresh G014: Conifer; very shallow, dry to fresh G023: Red pine-white pine conifer; very shallow, humid G025: Hemlock-cedar conifer; very shallow, humid G026: Conifer; very shallow, humid
Rich sites	5050: *Thuja occidentalis*; limestone bedrock, woodland 5251: *Acer spicatum, Thuja occidentalis, Betula papyriferal Taxus canadensis*; shrubland 6093: *Thuja occidentalisl Oligoneuron album*; woodland 5172: *Thuja occidentalis*; carbonate talus, woodland	FE30: Sugar maple, yellow birch; very thin soils MJ10: Yellow birch, fir, sugar maple; very thin soils MJ20: Yellow birch, fir; very thin soils MS10: Fir, yellow birch; very thin soils RT10: Hemlock; very thin soils	G028: Mixed-wood; very shallow, humid

S2 UPLAND: Stands on Dry or Fresh Deep Soils

	North American Associations	Quebec Classification	Ontario Classification
S2.1. Softwood stands on well drained soils			
Poor sites	6411: *Thuja occidentalisl Gaylussacia baccata, Vaccinium angustifolium*; woodland	RB12: Fir, white birch, or cedar from agriculture on deep loamy dry or fresh soils RB13: Fir, white birch, or cedar from agriculture on deep clayed dry or fresh soils RS11: Fir, cedar; deep coarse dry or fresh soils RE22: Black spruce with feathermoss or ericaceous shrubs on deep loamy dry or fresh soils	G036: Hemlock-cedar conifer; dry, sandy G037: Spruce-fir conifer; dry, sandy G038: Conifer; dry, sandy

[a] The four-digit number refers to the last four digits of the U.S. National Vegetation Classification Code, i.e., CEGL 00xxxx.

	North American Associations (98)	Quebec Classification (Ecological types) (52-56)	Ontario Classification (Ecosites) (3)
S2.1. Softwood stands on well drained soils (continued)			
Typical sites	2449: *Thuja occidentalis/ Abies balsamea, Acer spicatum*; forest	MS21: Fir, white birch; deep coarse dry or fresh soils MS22: Fir, white birch; deep loamy dry or fresh soils MS23: Fir, white birch; deep clayed dry or fresh soils MS61: Fir, red maple; deep coarse dry or fresh soils MS62: Fir, red maple; deep loamy dry or fresh soils MS63: Fir, red maple; deep clayed dry or fresh soils RS12: Fir, cedar; deep loamy dry or fresh soils RS13: Fir, cedar; deep clayed dry or fresh soils RS21: Fir, black spruce; deep coarse dry or fresh soils RS22: Fir, black spruce; deep loamy dry or fresh soils RS23: Fir, black spruce; deep clayed dry or fresh soils RS51: Fir, red spruce; deep coarse dry or fresh soils RS52: Fir, red spruce; deep loamy dry or fresh soils RS53: Fir, red spruce; deep clayed dry or fresh soils RT11: Hemlock; deep coarse dry or fresh soils RT12: Hemlock; deep loamy dry or fresh soils	G050: Pine-black spruce conifer; dry to fresh, coarse G052: Spruce-fir conifer; dry to fresh, coarse **Richer sites** G051: Hemlock-cedar conifer; dry to fresh, coarse G053: Conifer; dry to fresh, coarse G083: Black spruce-pine conifer; fresh, clayey G084: Hemlock-cedar conifer; fresh, clayey G086: Conifer; fresh, clayey G097: Red pine-white pine conifer; fresh, silty to fine loamy G099: Pine-black spruce conifer; fresh, silty to fine loamy G100: Hemlock-cedar conifer; fresh, silty to fine loamy G101: Spruce-fir conifer; fresh, silty to fine loamy G102: Conifer; fresh, silty to fine loamy
S2.2. Tolerant mixed-wood and hardwood stands on well drained soils			
Rich sites – mixed-wood stands	2595: *Thuja occidentalis (Betula alleghaniensis, Tsuga canadensis)*; forest	MJ11: Yellow birch, fir, and sugar maple; deep coarse dry or fresh soils MJ12: Yellow birch, fir, and sugar maple; deep loamy dry or fresh soils MJ13: Yellow birch, fir, and sugar maple; deep clayed dry or fresh soils MJ21: Yellow birch, fir; deep coarse dry or fresh soils MJ22: Yellow birch, fir; deep loamy dry or fresh soils MJ23: Yellow birch, fir; deep clayed dry or fresh soils	

	North American Associations (98)	Quebec Classification (Ecological types) (52-56)	Ontario Classification (Ecosites) (3)
S2.2. Tolerant mixed-wood and hardwood stands on well drained soils (continued)			
Rich sites – mixed-wood stands (continued)		MS11: Fir, yellow birch; deep coarse dry or fresh soils MS12: Fir, yellow birch; deep loamy dry or fresh soils MS13: Fir, yellow birch; deep clayed dry or fresh soils RP11: Red or white pine; deep coarse dry or fresh soils RP12: Red or white pine; deep loamy dry or fresh soils	
Rich sites – hardwood stands	6508: *Thuja occidentalis, Fraxinus pennsylvanical Acer pensylvanicum*; woodland	FE12: Sugar maple, bitternut hickory; deep loamy dry or fresh soils FE22: Sugar maple, basswood; deep loamy dry or fresh soils FE31: Sugar maple, yellow birch; deep coarse dry or fresh soils FE32: Sugar maple, yellow birch; deep loamy dry or fresh soils FE33: Sugar maple, yellow birch; deep clayed dry or fresh soils FE52: Sugar maple, ironwood; deep loamy dry or fresh soils FE62: Sugar maple, red oak; deep loamy dry or fresh soils	G120: Ash-elm; moist, fine

S3 LOWLAND: Stands on Moist Deep Mineral Soils

	North American Associations (98)	Quebec Classification (Ecological types) (52-56)	Ontario Classification (Ecosites) (3)
S3.1. Softwood stands on imperfectly drained soil			
Poor sites	6361: *Picea mariana, Picea rubens/Pleurozium schreberi*; forest	RS24: Fir, black spruce; deep coarse moist soils RS25: Fir, black spruce; deep loamy moist soils RS26: Fir, black spruce; deep clayed moist soils RS54: Fir, red spruce; deep coarse moist soils RS55: Fir, red spruce; deep loamy moist soils RS56: Fir, red spruce; deep clayed moist soils RE24: Black spruce with feathermoss or ericaceous shrubs on deep coarse moist soils RE25: Black spruce with feathermoss or ericaceous shrubs on deep loamy moist soils RE26: Black spruce with feathermoss or ericaceous shrubs on deep clayed moist soils	G068: Conifer; moist, coarse

	North American Associations (98)	Quebec Classification (Ecological types) (52-56)	Ontario Classification (Ecosites) (3)
S3.1. Softwood stands on imperfectly drained soil (continued)			
Typical sites	6199: *Thuja occidentalis, Acer rubrum/Cornus sericea*; forest 6175: *Thuja occidentalis (Picea rubens)/ Tiarella cordifolia*; forest	MS24: Fir, white birch; deep coarse moist soils MS25: Fir, white birch; deep loamy moist soils MS26: Fir, white birch; deep clayed moist soils RB15: Fir, white birch or cedar from agriculture on deep loamy moist soils RB16: Fir, white birch or cedar from agriculture on deep clayed moist soils RS14: Fir, cedar; deep coarse moist soils RS15: Fir ,cedar; deep loamy moist soils RS16: Fir, cedar; deep clayed moist soils	G066: Hemlock-cedar conifer; moist, coarse G113: White pine conifer; moist, fine G115: Hemlock-cedar conifer; moist, fine G116: Spruce-fir conifer; moist, fine G117: Conifer; moist, fine
S3.2. Tolerant mixed-wood and hardwoods stands on imperfectly drained soils			
Rich sites	2450: *Thuja occidentalis, Betula alleghaniensis*; forest 2595: *Thuja occidentalis (Betula alleghaniensis, Tsuga canadensis)*; forest	FE35: Sugar maple, yellow birch; deep loamy moist soils FE36: Sugar maple, yellow birch; deep clayed moist soils MJ14: Yellow birch, fir, and sugar maple; deep coarse moist soils MJ15: Yellow birch, fir, and sugar maple; deep loamy moist soils MJ16: Yellow birch, fir, and sugar maple; deep clayed moist soils MJ24: Yellow birch, fir; deep coarse moist soils MJ25: Yellow birch, fir; deep loamy moist soils MJ26: Yellow birch, fir; deep clayed moist soils MS15: Fir, yellow birch; deep loamy moist soils MS16: Fir, yellow birch; deep clayed moist soils MF14: Black ash, fir; deep coarse moist soils MF15: Black ash, fir; deep loamy moist soils MF16: Black ash, fir; deep clayed moist soils RT14: Hemlock; deep coarse moist soils RT15: Black ash, fir; deep loamy moist soils	G070: Aspen-birch hardwood; moist, coarse G071: Elm-ash hardwood; moist, coarse G073: Sugar maple hardwood; moist, coarse G074: Red maple hardwood; moist, coarse G119: Birch hardwood; moist, fine G124: Maple hardwood; moist, fine

S4 LOWLAND: Stands on Very Moist Deep Mineral or Organic Soils

	North American Associations (98)	Quebec Classification (Ecological types) (52-56)	Ontario Classification (Ecosites) (3)
S4.1. Softwood stands on poorly drained soils			
Poor sites (with no ground water circulation)	2456: *Thuja occidentalis* (*Picea mariana, Abies balsamea*)/ *Alnus incana*; forest 5225: *Thuja occidentalis, Larix laricina*/ *Sphagnum* spp.; forest 6007: *Thuja occidentalis*/ *Sphagnum* (*girgensohnii, warnstorfii*); forest 6363: *Chamaecyparis thyoides, Picea rubens*/*Gaylussacia baccata*/*Gaultheria hispidula*; forest 6321: *Chamaecyparis thyoides*/ *Chamaedaphne calyculata*; woodland	RE37: Black spruce with sphagnum on mineral ombrotrophic very moist soils RE39: Black spruce with sphagnum on organic ombrotrophic very moist soils RS37: Fir, black spruce with sphagnum on mineral ombrotrophic very moist soils RS39: Fir, black spruce with sphagnum on organic ombrotrophic very moist soils RB19: Fir, white birch, or cedar from agriculture on organic ombrotrophic very moist soils	G128: Organic intermediate conifer swamp G223: Mineral intermediate conifer swamp
Rich sites (with ground water circulation)	2455: *Thuja occidentalis* (*Larix laricina*); seepage forest 6507: *Thuja occidentalis, Abies balsamea*/ *Ledum groenlandicum*/ *Carex trisperma*; woodland	RC38: Cedar on mineral or organic minerotrophic very moist soils RE38: Black spruce with sphagnum on mineral or organic minerotrophic very moist soils RS18: Fir, cedar on mineral or organic minerotrophic very moist soils RS38: Fir, black spruce with sphagnum on mineral or organic minerotrophic very moist soils	G129: Organic rich conifer swamp G224: Mineral rich conifer swamp
S4.2. Mixed-wood and hardwood stands on poorly drained soils			
Rich sites (with ground water circulation)	5165: *Thuja occidentalis, Fraxinus nigra*; forest	FO18: Elm, black ash; mineral or organic minerotrophic very moist soils FE38: Sugar maple, yellow birch; mineral or organic minerotrophic very moist soils MF18: Black ash, fir; mineral or organic minerotrophic very moist soils MJ18: Yellow birch, fir, and sugar maple; mineral or organic minerotrophic very moist soils MJ28: Yellow birch, fir; mineral or organic minerotrophic very moist soils MS18: Fir, yellow birch; mineral or organic minerotrophic very moist soils	G130: Intolerant hardwood swamp G131: Maple hardwood swamp G133: Hardwood swamp

Even-age Stands[8]

Cleaning

Cleaning is a release treatment made in an age class not past the sapling stage to free the favored trees from less desirable individuals of the same age class that overtop them or are likely to do so (130).

Clearcutting

Clearcutting is the cutting of essentially all trees, producing a fully exposed microclimate for the development of a new age class. Regeneration can be from natural seeding, direct seeding, planted seedlings, or advance reproduction. Groups, strips, or patches (group, strip or patch clearcutting) may be left uncut. The management unit or stand in which regeneration, growth, and yield are regulated consists of the individual clearcut stand. When the primary source of regeneration is advance reproduction, the preferred term is overstory removal (130).

Commercial thinning

Thinning is a made to reduce stand density to improve the growth of residual stems, enhance forest health, or recover potential mortality. Commercial thinning refers to any type of thinning done to produce merchantable material at least equal to the value of the direct costs of harvesting (130).

Crown thinning

Removal of trees from the dominant and codominant crown classes to favor the best trees of those same crown classes (synonym: thinning from above, high thinning) (114).

Precommercial thinning

The removal of submerchantable trees not for immediate financial return but to reduce stocking to concentrate growth on the more desirable trees (130).

Seed tree thinning

Seed tree thinning refers to the cutting of all trees except for a small number of widely dispersed trees retained for seed production and to produce a new age class in a fully exposed microenvironment. Seed trees may be removed after regeneration is established (130).

Shelterwood

Shelterwood refers to the cutting of trees, leaving healthy main canopy trees needed to produce sufficient shade and seedfall to produce a new age class in a moderated microenvironment. The sequence of treatments can include three types of cuttings: (a) a preparatory cut to enhance conditions for seed production—which is not usually required for cedar; (b) a regeneration cut to prepare the seed bed and to create a new age class; and (c) a removal cut to release established regeneration from competition with the overwood; cutting may be done uniformly throughout the stand (uniform shelterwood), in groups or patches (group shelterwood), or in strips (strip shelterwood). In the variant **Shelterwood with reserves**, some or all of the shelter trees are retained after regeneration has become established to attain goals other than regeneration (such as ecological legacies) or as a means of ensuring a local seed source if regeneration fails with the first sequence of treatments (130).

---

[8] Of a forest, stand, or forest type, in which relatively small age differences exist between individual trees. Differences are generally not to exceed 20 to 25 percent of the target rotation age (19, 130).

Thinning from below

Removal of trees from the lower crown classes to favor those in the upper crown classes (synonym: low thinning) (114).

Uneven-age Stands[9]

Uneven-age methods regenerate and maintain a multi-age structure by removing some trees in all size classes either singly, in small groups, or in strips (130).

Irregular shelterwood system

The irregular shelterwood system is similar to the regular or uniform shelterwood system, with the difference that the dominant canopy is removed after a long (and sometimes indefinite) period of time by one or more harvests. This can be done by sequentially regenerating groups or patches in the stands (rather the whole stand in the same treatment) or by performing a single uniform partial cutting and letting a very long regeneration period occur before the final harvest (114).

The irregular shelterwood system is an uneven-age system, without a goal of sustained and constant production of goods and services at the stand level, such as the selection system. Sustainable production can be reached alternatively at the forest management unit, such as in the case of the even-age regime.

---

[9] A forest, stand, or forest type in which intermingling trees differ markedly in age. The differences in age permitted in an uneven-age stand are usually greater than 10-20 years. Usually form more than three distinct age classes (19).

Selection cutting

Two types of selection cuttings are distinguished (130):

*   Single-tree selection: individual trees of all size classes are removed more or less uniformly throughout the stand to promote growth of remaining trees and to provide space for regeneration (synonym: individual tree selection).

*   Group selection: trees are removed and new age classes are established in small groups. The width of groups is commonly about twice the height of the mature trees with smaller openings providing microenvironments suitable for tolerant regeneration and larger openings providing conditions suitable for more intolerant regeneration. The management unit or stand in which regeneration, growth, and yield are regulated consists of an aggregation of groups. Strip and patch selection cutting variants also exist.

The selection system is an uneven-age regime that aims to provide a sustained and constant production of goods and services at the stand level (101, 123).

Even-age or Uneven-age

Improvement cutting

The removal of less desirable trees of any species in a stand of poles or larger trees, primarily to improve composition and timber quality (synonym: tending) (130).

Management Objectives and Priorities

Wood production (specify) _____ ❏   Wildlife habitat _____ ❏

Nontimber forest products _____ ❏   Biodiversity _____ ❏

Native American values _____ ❏   Aesthetics _____ ❏

Other _____ ❏

Cedar:

Desired amount of cedar in regeneration (stems/ac, stocking)   _____

Target maximum d.b.h. or target rotation   _____

Number of trees to be retained for biodiversity (reserves, snags)   _____

Problems (to be completed after stand description)

Immediate need for action?   ❏   Quality problems   ❏

  Maturity   ❏   Low vigor   ❏

  Sanitation   ❏   Poor site productivity   ❏

  Overstocked   ❏   Stand structure problems (specify) _____ ❏

  Need for regeneration   ❏   Competition (specify species) _____ ❏

Low expected harvest revenues   ❏   Fragility (erosion, windthrow, scalping) _____ ❏

Market constraints   ❏   Trafficability problems (slope, wet, solidity) _____ ❏

Other problems or comments:

Cedar:

Risk of seedling water stress   ❏   Need for scarification   ❏

Advance growth to protect when harvesting   ❏   Need for understory competition control   ❏

Poor current growth vs. past growth   ❏   Poor current growth vs. site potential   ❏

Sufficient shelter for cedar growth or establishment   ❏   Excessive browsing   ❏

Possible Solutions

	Remaining
1) No action, delay treatment until _____	❑

For regeneration (if needed)

2) Scarification of entire surface	❑
3) Scarification of a part of the surface and protect advance regeneration	❑
4)	❑

For tending saplings or poles

5) Control spacing	❑
6) Eliminate competition with herbicides	❑
7) Mechanical removal of competition	❑
8)	❑

For harvesting

9) Adjust spacing to optimize cedar growth (and other quality trees)	❑
10) Cut poor quality and low vigor trees	❑
11) Cut mature trees	❑
12) Keep a residual cover of 60-70%	❑
13)	❑

For stand structure

14) Two-story stand	❑
15) Irregular structure	❑
16) Balanced structure (shade-tolerant species needed)	❑
17) Even-age stand	❑
18)	❑

Drop Unsuitable Options and Justify Remaining Options

Solutions

\# _____ Too much effort compared to the gains

\# _____ Ecologically unacceptable (e.g., erosion…)

\# _____ Too risky

\# _____ Violates the financial constraints

\# _____ Inconsistent with objectives (specify)

Options selected: _____

Justification:

Silvicultural Prescription

Silvicultural system:

Treatment:

Pattern (uniform, strip, group):

Requirements:

Mitigation measures:

Evaluate the Results

Required follow up

When evaluation is to be conducted:

Type of evaluation:

   Regeneration   ❏

   Level of competition (species and height):   ❏

   Growth   ❏

   Vigor   ❏

   Windthrow   ❏